TRAGEDY

TRAGEDY

TERRY EAGLETON

YALE UNIVERSITY PRESS
NEW HAVEN AND LONDON

For information about this and other Yale University Press publications, please contact:
U.S. Office: sales.press@yale.edu   yalebooks.com
Europe Office: sales@yaleup.co.uk   yalebooks.co.uk

Typeset in Adobe Garamond Pro by IDSUK (DataConnection) Ltd
Printed in Great Britain by TJ International Ltd, Padstow, Cornwall

Library of Congress Control Number: 2020937960

ISBN 978-0-300-25221-7

A catalogue record for this book is available from the British Library.

10 9 8 7 6 5 4 3 2 1

In Memory of Nora Bartlett

CONTENTS

Preface   *viii*

1   Did Tragedy Die?   1

2   Incest and Arithmetic   40

3   Tragic Transitions   56

4   Fruitful Falsehoods   99

5   The Inconsolable   155

Notes   *221*

Index   *235*

PREFACE

This is the second study of tragedy I have written, perhaps because there are few other places where great art and the most fundamental moral and political issues are so closely interlocked. One reason why tragedy matters is that it is a measure of what we ultimately value; but another is that a certain ideology has appropriated the form, rendering it suspect to a good many people who might otherwise reap value from it. It is the aristocrat of art-forms, and my own work, both in *Sweet Violence* and in this book, represents an attempt in the manner of my late friend and teacher Raymond Williams to democratise it.

Why tragedy matters to me personally is a more elusive affair. If, like Williams's *Modern Tragedy*, I am interested among other things in the relations between tragedy in art and tragedy in everyday life, it may be because I embarked on the study of tragic art at Cambridge under the shadow of a real-life calamity, the death of my father, which I describe in my memoir *The Gatekeeper*. If a certain vein of tragedy draws life from death, though not without grief and guilt, this was the condition in which I first approached the subject as a student and in diminished form the way in which I encounter it today.

So I have been thinking about tragedy for well over half a century, ever since Jan Marsh, now a distinguished Pre-Raphaelite scholar, remarked to me after we had both sat the Tragedy paper in the Cambridge University English Tripos that 'the examiners seem to think that tragedy is a good thing'. With that simple but pregnant remark, one of which she almost certainly has no recollection, she planted a seed of which much of my work on tragedy has been the fruit. For that, I am deeply grateful to her.

T.E.

1

DID TRAGEDY DIE?

It wasn't a thing of monstrous order; not a fate rare
and distinguished; not a stroke of fortune that
overwhelmed and immortalised; it had only the
stamp of the common doom.

(Henry James, 'The Beast in the Jungle')

Tragedy is said to be universal, which is true enough if one has
the everyday sense of the word in mind. Grieving over the
death of a child, a mining disaster or the gradual disintegration of a human mind is not confined to any particular culture.
Sorrow and despair constitute a lingua franca. Yet tragedy in
the artistic sense is a highly specific affair. There is no close
equivalent of it, for example, in the traditional art of China,
India or Japan.[1] In a superb study of early-modern tragedy,
Blair Hoxby points out that 'Europeans once lived without

any category of *the* tragic, though they saw tragedies every-where around them.'[2] The form originates not as a timeless reflection on the human condition, but as a form in which a particular civilisation grapples for a fleeting historical moment with the conflicts which beset it.[3]

All art has a political dimension, but tragedy actually began life as a political institution. Indeed, for Hannah Arendt it is the political art *par excellence*.[4] Only in theatre, she writes, 'is the political sphere of human life transposed into art'.[5] In fact, ancient Greek tragedy is not only a political institution in itself, but two of its works, Aeschylus's *Eumenides* and Sophocles' *Oedipus at Colonus*, concern the founding or securing of public institutions. It is a familiar fact that tragic drama, performed in ancient Greece as part of the festival of Dionysus, was funded by an individual appointed by the city state, whose public duty was to train and pay the Chorus. The state supervised the proceedings in a general way under the authority of the chief magistrate, and held the scripts of the performances in its archives. Actors were paid by the *polis*, and the state also provided a fund to pay the entrance fee for citizens too poor to pay it themselves.[6] The judges of the competition were elected by the body of citizens, and would no doubt have brought to bear on the dramatic performances the critical acumen they were accustomed to exercising as jurors in the law courts and members of the political assembly. As Jean-Pierre Vernant and Pierre Vidal-Naquet comment, it was a question of 'the city turning itself into a theatre'.[7] 'The text of tragedy,' remarks Rainer Friedrich, 'becomes part of the larger text of the civil discourse of the *polis*.'[8]

Tragedy, then, was not only an aesthetic experience or dramatic spectacle. It was also a form of ethico-political education which helped to inculcate civic virtue. For Hannah Arendt, there is a parallel between politics and tragic theatre, since when the former is conducted in full public session, as in ancient Athens, it turns its participants into performers akin to actors on a stage.[9] Later tragedy is not for the most part an official political institution, though in eighteenth-century Germany Goethe's novel *Wilhelm Meister* and the dramatic theory of Gotthold Lessing reflect on the need for a state theatre which will unify the nation. For Lessing, as for some other German thinkers of his age, the theatre fosters public virtue and a sense of corporate identity.[10] Whether nationally based or not, however, tragic drama continues to deal with affairs of state, revolts against authority, thrusting ambition, court intrigues, violations of justice, struggles for sovereignty, all of which tend to centre on the careers of high-born figures whose lives and deaths have momentous consequences for society as a whole.

Politically speaking, Greek tragedy had a double role, both validating social institutions and calling them into question. Art may legitimate a social order through its content, but also by providing its audience with a psychological safety-valve, fostering harmless fantasies which might distract them from the more unsavoury aspects of the regimes under which they live. Aristotle's *Poetics* does not view tragedy as harmless fantasy, but it does regard it as feeding its audience strictly controlled doses of certain emotions (pity and fear) which might otherwise prove socially disruptive. It is, in short, a form of political homeopathy.[11] As far as tragedy as critique is concerned, it is astonishing that an official political event, part of a revered religious festival, could shine so bold a light on the dark subtext of ancient Greek civilisation – on madness, parricide, incest, infanticide and the like, however prudently these matters were thrust into the mythological past. It is as if a pageant in honour of the Queen of England were to present a series of tableaux from the adultery of Lancelot and Guinevere to the exploits of Jack the Ripper.

In Aristotle's view, Greek tragedy can provide a form of public therapy, purging an emotional flabbiness that might endanger the health of the *polis*. Like Plato, however, you can also see certain aspects of the theatre as politically subversive and demand its strict regulation by the state. Later tragedy has a range of political roles. It can remind its audience of how sickeningly precarious the power of the mighty can be, or provide a body of mythology around which the nation may be reborn. We shall see later how German philosophy of tragedy sets out to resolve certain contradictions which spring from an early stage of middle-class civilisation. The public or political dimension of tragedy lives on in the theatre of Henrik Ibsen, even if the setting of his drama is for the most part domestic. This is because the family in Ibsen serves as a medium for deeper social issues, so that private and public domains become hard to dissociate. It is only after this point that we encounter on a sizeable scale what might be called private tragedy, foreshadowed in some domestic drama in the eighteenth century in which what is primarily at stake is an incestuous father, a drug-addicted mother or a married couple who survive by tearing one another apart.

The politics of tragedy, however, involves more than what happens on stage. It also means a struggle over the meaning of the tragic itself. In his study *The Death of Tragedy*, the critic George Steiner sees tragedy as a critique of modernity. The truly tragic spirit expires with the birth of the modern. It cannot survive an era which places its faith in secular values, an enlightened politics, the rational conduct of human affairs and the ultimate intelligibility of the universe. It is ill at ease in this disenchanted world, so that the term 'modern tragedy' becomes something of an oxymoron. Tragedy cannot tolerate a utilitarian ethics or an egalitarian politics. As an aristocrat among art-forms, it serves among other things as a memory trace of a more spiritually exalted social order at the heart of a distastefully prosaic epoch. It represents a residue of transcendence in an age of materialism.

What began life as a political institution, then, ends up as a form of anti-politics. We are rescued from the clutches of the merchant, clerk and local councillor and restored to a world of gods, martyrs, heroes and warriors. In the debased age of the common people, we can turn once again to mystery, mythology and the metaphysical. Given the historical affinity between tragedy and democracy, this aversion to the democratic spirit is especially ironic. Tragedy, or at least a partisan version of it, ranks among the various surrogates for religion in the modern period, dealing as it does with guilt, transgression, suffering, redemption and glorification.[12] It is with the death of God that tragic art is reborn, with all the majestic aura of the divinity it replaces. For much aesthetic theory, there can be nothing more resplendent than the sublime, of which tragedy is the supreme expression – which is to say that tragedy is doubly distinguished, occupying the highest rank of the highest aesthetic mode.

On this view, which is by no means confined to the work of Steiner, tragic drama is everything that the modern age is not: elitist rather than egalitarian, blue-blooded rather than horny-handed, spiritual rather than scientific, absolute rather than contingent, irremediable rather than reparable, universal rather than parochial, a question of destiny rather than self-determination. It deals with the death of princes rather than the suicide of salesmen. Arthur Schopenhauer is one of the rare philosophers of tragedy who insists that a great misfortune, which in his mildly heterodox view is enough to constitute a tragic action, can happen to anyone regardless of social rank. This mishap, he comments, need not be caused by rare circumstances or monstrous characters, but can arise easily, spontaneously, out of routine human behaviour. Yet though he holds that everyday tragedies are the finest in the sense that more of us can identify with them, he also claims rather inconsistently that tragic protagonists should preferably be of patrician status, since their fall makes more of a splash. The circumstances which plunge a middle-class family into penury and despair, Schopenhauer observes, may seem trifling in the eyes of the mighty, and since they can be easily remedied by human action are unlikely to move them to pity.[13]

The French naturalistic novelists Edmond and Jules de Goncourt are rather more generous-minded. They write:

> We must ask ourselves whether in this era of equality in which we live there could still be, for writer or for reader, any classes too unworthy, any miseries too low, any dramas too foul-mouthed, any catastrophes insufficiently noble in their terror. We became curious to know whether Tragedy, the conventional form of a forgotten literature and a vanished society, was really dead; whether in a country lacking castes and legal aristocracy the misfortunes of the little people and the poor could arouse interest, emotion, and pity to the same degree as the misfortunes of the great and rich; whether, in a word, the tears that are shed below could evoke tears as readily as those which are shed on high.[14]

In this respect, the Goncourts are heirs to the lineage of so-called bourgeois tragedy, which for such eighteenth-century figures as Diderot and Lessing presents us with ordinary men and women in familiar situations. In Lessing's view, the middle-class spectators in the stalls should find themselves reflected in the characters on stage.[15] For this current of thought, tragedy is to be defined neither by a heroic tone, neo-classical conventions nor the social status of its characters, but by its emotional authenticity. Medieval and Renaissance tragic theory see the fall of a high-born hero from prosperity to misery as crucial to the form; but once protagonists are stolidly bourgeois rather than glamorously aristocratic, the notion of tragedy as a calamitous fall begins to fade. So does the idea of it as exposing the precariousness of power or the mutability of human affairs.

For a more traditional view than Lessing's, tragic art is a matter not of the misfortunes of the poor but of myth and fate, ritual and blood sacrifice, high crimes and heroic expiation, evil and redemption, jealous gods and submissive victims. The suffering it portrays is ennobling as well as appalling, so that we leave the theatre edified by scenes of carnage.[16] Only when confronted by calamity is the human spirit able to reveal its true nobility. Tragedy is that peculiar form which presents us neither simply with human affliction nor simply with what transcends it, but with each in terms of the other. In Steiner's words, it represents 'a fusion of grief and joy, of lament over the fall of man and of rejoicing in the resurrection of his spirit'.[17] Artistic form plays a vital role here, shaping, distancing, purifying and condensing the tragic materials in a way that makes their power to appal us more acceptable. David Hume remarks in his essay 'Of Tragedy' that the eloquence and artistry of tragic art renders its harrowing contents more pleasurable. Edmund Burke spins the ingenious argument that this pleasure is Nature's way of stopping us from shunning real-life scenes of wretchedness, inspiring us instead to fly to the aid of those involved.[18] Besides, to fictionalise events is to invest them with an intelligibility, as well as a potential universality, that they may lack in everyday life. In ancient Greek tragedy, pushing the action back into a legendary past may achieve much the same cognitive distance. For all the chaos and chanciness of the tragic action, we can dimly discern the workings of providence within it, not least if we stand a little way off.

In the view of some modern critics, philosophers such as Hegel gentrify the unspeakable by insisting that tragedy discloses a rational design. It is a persuasive case, though the very fact that tragic art exists suggests that there is more to the world than pain. Tragedy is not a cry without words. The trauma of the Real for Jacques Lacan lies beyond language, but tragedy remains just on this side of that silence. 'Language by means of sounds, or better still words, is a vast liberation,' writes Bertolt Brecht, 'because it means the sufferer is beginning to produce something. He's already mixing his sorrow with an account of the blows he has received; he's already making something out of the utterly devastating. Observation has set in.'[19] In tragedy, remarks Roland Barthes in *On Racine*, one never dies because one is always talking. True despair happens when we are no longer capable of speech. If there is hope after the death of Lear, it is inscribed – among other places – in the very integrity of the verse, which fails to fall silent in the face of this catastrophe. Yet the fact that the poetry does not unravel at the seams is small recompense for the horrors it portrays. 'Every work of art, including tragedy,' remarks Boris Pasternak's Yuri Zhivago, 'witnesses to the joy of existence. . . . It is always meditating upon death, and it is always thereby creating life.' But the fulfilments of art in no sense redeem the suffering the novel portrays.

On a conservative view, Aeschylus is tragic but Auschwitz is not. It is not that the Holocaust is not lamentable beyond words, but that it does nothing to enhance our sense of human possibility. Whatever leaves us dejected rather than exalted – an air crash, a famine, the death of a child – fails to qualify for tragic status. The aesthetic sense of the word drifts free of its everyday meaning. It is a historical rift as well as a conceptual one: the ancient Greeks would seem to have little idea of the tragic in our own colloquial sense of the term, or for that matter of tragedy as a world-view (though Sophocles' grim pronounce-ment that it would be better for men and women never to have been born has all the resonance of one). For ancient Greece, the term might evoke the magnificent or grandiose, which is why

Aristophanes can poke fun at tragedy's high style, but rarely the sorrowful.[20] The term 'tragic' in its common-or-garden sense is a later development and as such is a case of life imitating art. It means something like 'unspeakably sad', as distinct from a form of art or vision of the world. It is worth noting, incidentally, that a culture can have a tragic vision without producing any very notable tragic art, or vice versa.

On the classical view, real-life disasters are not tragic because they are a matter of raw suffering. It is only when that suffering is shaped and distanced by art, so that something of its deeper significance is released, that we can properly speak of tragedy. Tragic art does more than portray the intolerable: it also invites us to reflect on it, honour it, memorialise it, investigate its causes, mourn its victims, absorb the experience into our everyday life, draw on its terrors to confront our own weakness and mortality and perhaps find some tentative moment of affirmation at its heart. That affirmation, as we have seen, may be simply the fact that art itself continues to be possible. The problem with this theory, however, is that these things may also happen in the case of real-life calamities, which are rarely a matter of suffering and nothing else. The attack on the World Trade Center in 2001 led swiftly to a collective drama of public mourning and meditation, myth and legend, naming and honouring, contemplation and commemoration, all of which were part of the tragic action. We do not need suffering to be put on stage in order to see past the immediate pain.

The conservative version of tragedy depends heavily on the theatre of ancient Greece, but fails to fit with some of its works. The drama of Euripides, for example, is hardly conspicuous for a view of the universe as lawful and harmonious. For conservative theories, such order grants us the consolation of meaning, and to show it being violated is to demonstrate how ultimately impregnable it is. It also fosters sentiments of reverence, awe and submission. Conscious of our frailty, we find in the tragic a critique of hubristic reason, without thereby selling the pass to pessimism or scientific determinism. We know ourselves to be free, but in a way which is compatible with a respect for cosmic necessity. If vulgar determinism is to be rejected, so is anarchic individualism. Human beings are neither the mere playthings of external forces, nor (as in a familiar middle-class mythology) free-standing and supremely self-responsible. They are free enough to refute the scientific materialists, but subject to cosmic law in a way which equally confounds the liberal individualists. Human powers are thus humbled and affirmed at a stroke. We are agents, to be sure, but not wholly the source of our own actions. There is a remote parallel here with the audience of a stage tragedy, which is active in the way it interprets the drama but physically passive and powerless, unable to intervene to avert the catastrophe and thus as much a victim of fate as the protagonists themselves. With a few avant-garde exceptions, all theatre is an image of determinism, given that the audience are not allowed to clamber on stage. The words 'theatre' and 'theory' are etymologically related, and both suggest contemplation rather than action.

Since we are able to pluck value from failure and desolation, there is hope, but not some bright-eyed optimism.[21] Both the pessimists and progressivists are accordingly outflanked. Human nobility is affirmed in the teeth of the mechanical materialists, but the utopian dreamers are reminded of human finitude. One must cling to the value tragedy reveals while also acknowledging its fragility, steering a course between cynicism and triumphalism. Reason has its place in human affairs, *pace* the subversive nihilists; but the enigma of suffering throws the limits of such reason into stark relief, a fact which yields no comfort to the middle-class rationalists. There is pity and fear, but these are uplifting emotions, not to be confused with some sentimental humanitarianism.

Tragedy, in this view, values wisdom over knowledge, mystery above lucidity, the eternal over the historical. It represents the dark underside of Enlightenment, the shadow cast by the *Aufklarers'* excess of light. 'The ethos of tragedy,' writes Christopher Norris, 'is something foreign to the general semantics of humanistic rationalism.'[22] Among its quarrels with the *illuminati* is its claim that the roots of tragedy lie deeper than the social, and are consequently beyond repair. No medication could cure Philoctetes' pus-swollen foot, no psychological counselling retrieve Phaedra from her doom. Marriage guidance could do nothing for Anna Karenina, or a course in cultural difference salvage the fortunes of Othello. Tragedy is thus a rebuff to the social reformists and political utopianists. In George Steiner's eyes, Ibsen's drama fails the test of tragedy because it turns on issues which can be practically redressed. *An Enemy of the People* takes as its subject the infection of a public bath-house, which in Steiner's view is far too ignoble an affair for genuine tragedy. 'If there are bathrooms in the houses of tragedy,' he writes with a splendid flourish, 'it is for Agamemnon to be murdered in.'[23]

On this theory, there is something intolerably callow about social hope, compared with the mature disenchantment of those who have peered into the dark heart of things.[24] 'The destiny of Lear,' Steiner declares, 'cannot be resolved by the establishment of adequate homes for the aged.'[25] It is not in fact obvious that this is so. If Lear, cast out by his flint-hearted daughters, had been granted solace and shelter by some kindlier soul, he might not have needed to die. All the same, William Empson has a point when he argues that 'it is only in degree that any improvement of society could prevent wastage of human powers; the waste even in a fortunate life, the isolation even of a life rich in intimacy, cannot but be felt deeply, and is the central feeling of tragedy'.[26] This need not be an anti-political case; in fact, Empson makes it as a life-long socialist. It is, however, to insist on the limits of the political. Politics may abolish certain conflicts, but it cannot put paid to all distress and despair.

On the traditional view, tragic art cannot survive long in a world bereft of myth, providence and the burdensome presence of the gods. Quite when it gives up the ghost, however, is a matter of dispute. Unlike Mark Twain, tragedy has been the subject not of one but of a whole series of premature obituaries. Hegel maintains that art as such has run its course in the modern era, and that though tragic drama continues to be staged it is for the most part inferior stuff, lacking the world-historical dimension of the ancients. It has turned from such momentous issues to ethics and psychology, a decline already prefigured in the work of Euripides. For Nietzsche, tragedy died in its infancy, strangled in its cradle with the advent of the sceptical Euripides and the cerebral Socrates. Sigmund Freud regards the idea of fate as vital to ancient tragedy, and doubts that there can be any convincing modern equivalent.[27] The Oedipus complex survives Oedipus himself, but some critics are less certain that tragedy does.

Richard Halpern rejects the 'death of tragedy' thesis, but argues with some plausibility that the form went on 'extended vacation' throughout the eighteenth and most of the nineteenth centuries.[28] One might add that this is the period in which an increasingly self-confident middle class is in the ascendant, and that it is when this assurance begins to falter, in the final decades of the nineteenth century, that tragedy stages a return. Steiner seems to claim that the art survives as late as Racine, but then begins to decline. Its waning, he maintains, 'was concomitant with the democratisation of Western ideals. . . . Tragedy argues an aristocracy of suffering, an excellence of pain.'[29] There are those for whom it is Christianity, with its eschatological vision of hope, which administers the *coup de grâce*, as well as studies such as Joseph Wood Krutch's *The Modern Temper*, for which the assassins in question are science and secularism. How tragic the death of tragedy is – whether its demise is to be mourned as a grievous loss – is a matter for debate. Reviewing Lionel Abel's *Metatheater: A New View of Dramatic Form*, Susan Sontag shares the author's view that the death of tragedy is not a cause for dismay, not least because in her view it was never a central current of Western theatre.[30]

Albert Camus regards the loss of a sense of order and constraint in modern times as fatal to the tragic spirit, which cannot thrive without individuals being grimly reminded of the limits of their powers.[31] Agnes Heller and Ferenc Feher see the end of tragedy as following hard on the heels of the death of God, rather than viewing the high style of tragedy as compensation for an absent deity. The modern world is the theatre of the *deus absconditus*, an ontological abyss into which tragic freedom and dignity have disappeared without trace.[32] There are also those for whom tragedy cannot survive the Holocaust, or the pervasive loss of meaning of late modernity, or the depthless, decentred subjectivity of postmodernism.[33] By contrast, Raymond Williams's *Modern Tragedy*, a riposte to

Steiner in its very title, sees tragic art as maintaining its vigour well into the twentieth century.

George Steiner upbraids both Christianity and Marxism for having a hand in the decline of tragedy. 'The least touch of any theology that has a compensating Heaven to offer the tragic hero is fatal,' he declares.[34] On this reckoning, one of the most moving tragic figures in English fiction – Samuel Richardson's Clarissa, who believes devoutly in an afterlife – is not tragic at all, and neither is Hamlet, if he really holds that felicity in the sense of paradise rather than merciful oblivion is where he is bound. Both Marxism and Christianity are fundamentally hopeful, whereas in Steiner's view tragedy ends badly. Yet this is surely doubtful. Aristotle speaks of a transition from misery to happiness as well as the reverse. The *Oresteia* ends on a positive note. A good deal of tragic drama mixes a strain of hope, however diffident and provisional, with its lamentation. What is tragic is not just a calamitous conclusion, as Steiner seems to imagine, but the fact that men and women must be hauled through hell in order to be redeemed; that many of them, such as Oedipus and Lear, will fail to survive this purgatorial process; and that, even if they do, there is no guarantee that they will emerge from it in sprightlier spiritual shape. Moreover, what is tragic is not simply this trauma of breaking and remaking, but the fact that it is necessary in the first place. Only because our humanity is so disfigured, and our self-delusion so deep-rooted, are such baptisms of fire essential. It would be better if the reformists were right and we could evolve into a future of justice and comradeship without the need for radical self-dispossession. Unfortunately, it is those who hold this view who are the true utopian fantasists, while the cold-eyed realists are those who see tragedy as an effort to gaze on the Medusa's head of the Real without being turned to stone.

Both Marxism and Christianity are indeed tragic doctrines, but this is not because they envisage a disastrous end to history. It is rather that they are conscious of the appalling price that an unjust world must pay for its redemption. The so-called New Testament is remarkable for being a tragic but not a heroic document. There is nothing in the least noble or edifying about the squalid death of its low-life protagonist, a death traditionally reserved by the Roman imperial power for political insurgents. Kathleen M. Sands writes that 'theistic faith is precisely the conviction that tragedy is only apparent, and that the losses told in tragedy are not really ultimate';[35] but, though suffering may be finally overcome, this can only come about if its reality is confronted, and it is this double optic which both the pessimists and the Panglossians fail to acknowledge. The risen body of Jesus, still bearing the marks of his wounds, cannot annul the fact of his torture and humiliation. Not even God can change the past. He cannot bring it about that those who died in torment actually expired in joy. It is true that

Christian faith holds out the promise of a future beyond tragedy – of a world in which whatever is broken will be made whole, those who mourn will be comforted and all tears will be wiped away; but only by a passage through death and self-abandonment can this future be attained.

As for Marx, those who claim that 'he repudiated the entire concept of tragedy'[36] overlook, among other things, his horror at the destruction of the English handloom weavers, which he sees as a profoundly tragic process, as well as his comment that capitalism emerges into existence dripping blood from every pore. Gilles Deleuze is thus mistaken to claim that 'Dialectics in general are not a tragic vision of the world but, on the contrary, the death of tragedy, the replacement of the tragic vision with a theoretical conception (with Socrates) or a Christian conception (with Hegel).'[37] Marx is a dialectician for whom the working through of conflict involves irreparable loss. Those who perished in the class struggle will not be requited by whatever successes their descendants are able to chalk up. In *Modern Tragedy*, Raymond Williams views the anti-colonial revolutions of the twentieth century as constituting a single tragic action extended in space and time; but by calling them tragic he does not mean that these insurrections were routed, or that it was folly to launch them in the first place. He means rather that the crimes of colonialism were so monstrous that resolving them involved a fight to the death, and that it is here that the tragedy lies.[38] That life should spring from death is not a cause for celebration, but it is preferable to there being no life at all.

The Steiner of *The Death of Tragedy* insists that tragedy implies value, even if it also puts it into question. We do not grieve over the loss of what we regard as worthless. The death of an earwig is not an occasion for Racinian rhetoric. Perhaps the ultimate tragedy would be a condition in which we were so careless of human value that we would no longer be able to mourn. '[Tragic] man,' Steiner comments, 'is ennobled by the vengeful spite or injustice of the gods. It does not make him innocent, but it hallows him as if he had passed through flame.'[39] In his later thought, however, any such exaltation spells the ruin of tragedy. Even Shakespeare, with the solitary exception of *Timon of Athens*, proves in this bleak view insufficiently gloomy to qualify for so-called 'absolute' tragic art in which 'nullity devours as does a black hole'.[40] But if tragedy must be absolute, what of those situations in which one's hopes might have been fulfilled but are actually frustrated? Is this not more poignant than a hope which is fruitless from the outset? Thomas Hardy's Jude Fawley dies in the awareness that there are plans afoot to establish a working men's college in the university that has shut him out, a fact which lends a keener edge to his own failure while at the same time qualifying any too-absolute despair.

There are, in fact, remarkably few tragedies of an unflinchingly nihilistic bent – certainly not *Timon*, unless one reads the play, absurdly, as endorsing its protagonist's crazed misanthropy; but in Steiner's eyes such instances of unremitting gloom are definitive of the form. The slightest flicker of positivity is likely to give comfort to the hard-nosed advocates of social engineering. He might have enlisted in his support the *Trauerspiel* playwrights examined in Walter Benjamin's *The Origin of German Tragic Drama*, who in a Europe ravaged by the Thirty Years War present human existence as vacuous and vain. Instead, he proposes Büchner's remorselessly cheerless *Woyzeck* as exemplary of the tragic mode, even though its protagonist is far from patrician, the kind of tragic hero Steiner generally prefers. The piece also dates from well after the time when *The Death of Tragedy* supposes tragedy to have expired, driven out by an unholy alliance of science, rationalism, secularism, democracy and the brutalising of language by a debased modernity. Profuse praise is also heaped on the work of Kleist, Hölderlin and Wagner, though like Büchner all three write after the moment when tragedy is said to have fallen silent.[41]

For the early Steiner, tragedy is dependent on a sense of cosmic order. In his later view, however, this no longer seems to be the case; instead, it confronts the reality of a barren world. It is an art which can accommodate no justice, recompense, providence or restitution. This, perhaps, is an excessive reaction to those for whom tragic art is essentially about reconciliation, a case we shall be looking at later. The problem, however, is that it identifies tragedy with pessimism – an equation scornfully rejected by the Nietzsche to whom Steiner is so deeply (if tacitly) indebted and one profoundly at odds with the tradition of tragic thought which he inherits. For that heritage, there is something to be gained in outflanking the callow optimists, but not at the cost of ditching all possibility of edification.

Steiner's conservatism thus leads him to argue two mutually incompatible cases, one early in his career and the other later. For the former Steiner, tragedy survives as long as men and women are forced to submit to the laws of some cosmic design; for the later Steiner, the world lacks all such providential pattern, and tragedy is the artistic form courageous enough to proclaim this dispiriting truth. Either way, the idea of tragedy issues a rebuke to the liberals and radicals – either because as philistine rationalists they reject all sense of mystery and transcendence or because they deludedly hold that there is enough meaning and value for the world to be feasibly changed. The case is inconsistent in other ways too. Of all modern dramatists, Samuel Beckett portrays the death of meaning more graphically than any other, but Steiner dismisses his work as crippled and monotonous. Besides, if any form of hope is inimical to the tragic spirit, why is Christian belief so central to the Renaissance context in which major tragedy blossomed?

Whether or not tragedy outlives the ancient Greeks depends, among other things, on what one means by the term. If Sophocles and Chekhov are tragic in quite different senses of the term, then the question of continuity is complicated. 'Tragedy,' writes Raymond Williams, 'is not a single and permanent kind of fact, but a series of experiences and conventions and institutions.'[42] If this is so, however, then we are bound to ask why we call all these experiences, conventions and institutions by the same name. Is the name all they have in common, or does it denote a single phenomenon? It is a quarrel between the nominalists and the essentialists, or the historicists and the universalists. Aristotle belongs to the latter camp in his belief that poetry is a more universal form than history, while others take a more historically relative view. Friedrich Hölderlin argues for an organic bond between ancient Greek tragedy and republicanism, convinced that only with the recreation of such political conditions might tragic art blossom afresh. The French Revolution thus holds out the possibility of its revival. In the meantime tragedy, in Hölderlin's view, has withered away. It has declined from its ancient grandeur into sentiment and sensationalism.[43] There is a sense in which the same is true for Karl Marx, who in the celebrated opening passage of *The Eighteenth Brumaire of Louis Bonaparte* sardonically contrasts the noble spirit of the ancient Roman republic with the tawdry attempts of modern bourgeois revolutionaries to tart themselves up in its garments. Driven to deceive themselves about the meagre content of their own insurrections, they strive in a mixture of farce and pathos 'to maintain their passion on the high plane of great historical tragedy'.[44]

In *The Origin of German Tragic Drama*, Walter Benjamin insists on the historical specificity of tragedy, arguing that only the ancient Greek variety truly deserves the name. The philosophy of tragedy, he complains, is a dehistoricising discourse, reducing tragedy to a generalised set of sentiments across quite different historical conditions. 'The tragic' does not exist. There is nothing in modern theatre remotely resembling Aeschylus or Sophocles. Seventeenth-century German *Trauerspiel*, by contrast, is explicitly bound to its historical context. In a study entitled *Hamlet or Hecuba?*, the philosopher Carl Schmitt is equally sceptical of a universalist view of the art, not least since the modern age is unequal to the task of producing it. The classical scholar Jean-Pierre Vernant insists that tragedy is peculiar to the ancient Greeks, and that only a century or so later Aristotle himself is incapable of truly understanding it.[45] Bernard Williams also regards tragedy as specific to ancient Greece, but suggests that our modern ethical notions come close to its vision of human life.[46] Theories of tragedy may also be part of their historical contexts: in Simon Goldhill's view, Hegel's philosophy of tragedy appeals to the collective norms and values of ancient Greek tragedy as a riposte to the abstract universalism and individualism of Immanuel Kant. 'For Hegel,' he maintains, 'tragedy is a doorway to rethinking Kant's notion of the subject.'[47] The German tragic theories we shall be examining later propose a universal idea of tragedy, yet this vision itself is the product of a unique historical moment.

It is possible to hold an essentialist view of tragedy while also claiming that, as a dramatic form, it has long since vanished. On this view, tragedy captures the reality of the human condition, but artistic and historical conditions are no longer hospitable to its representation on stage. If tragedy is part of the human spirit in general, then it is hard to see how it can die; but it may only manifest itself artistically at certain key historical moments. It is possible, however, that the choice between historicism and universalism, or nominalism and essentialism, is unnecessary. Perhaps it is true, *pace* the essentialists, that there is no single feature that all tragedies share. Not all the works we call tragic present us with a malevolent destiny or the downfall of the mighty, a fatal flaw or intimations of the Absolute, an exaltation of the spirit or an absent God. Yet there are enough overlapping threads and family resemblances among so-called tragic works for the nominalist case to be equally implausible. No doubt all the texts we call tragic do have one feature in common, namely some kind of affliction or adversity, and to this extent the essentialists are right. Even Raymond Williams, having cast doubt on the idea of a tragic essence in one study, modifies his position in another, arguing that 'the concept of tragedy still represents a reasonable though difficult grouping of works in a certain mode around death and extreme suffering and disintegration'.[48] But the diversity of such suffering reduces it to the slimmest of common denominators, which in turn should satisfy the most ardent culturalist or historicist. Besides, comedy is no stranger to pain and distress, as Shylock and Malvolio can attest.

Tragedy, in the everyday sense of failure and breakdown, is indeed universal. Not even the most utopian of social orders would be untouched by mortal injuries, baffled desires and broken relationships. The price of rejecting a view of tragedy as the death of princes for a more workaday sense of the term is that certain kinds of tragedy then become irreparable, which may not be the case if it is confined to the affairs of an elite. Princes may cease to wage warfare, but there is no apparent terminus to heartache or sexual jealousy. One may strip the tragic of its privilege, then, but only at the cost of accepting that some of it is here to stay. Cancer will no doubt be cured, but death will not. Perhaps we should hesitate before wishing for a life beyond tragedy, since one of the surest ways to attain it would be to lose our sense of value. Yet, even if there will always be ruined hopes and irreversible injuries, it does not follow that there is an unbroken lineage of art which dramatises these things in much the same way; and we have already noted that tragic art is by no means common to all civilisations.

The question, then, is whether tragedy dies or simply mutates. With the emergence of middle-class society, the focus begins to shift from a collective action to the individual hero. For Friedrich Schelling, as we shall see later, the tragic action is internalised, psychologised and individualised, in a way at odds with the ancient Greek theatre to which he believes himself to be faithful. What for Aristotle is a matter of action is for Schelling a question of consciousness. The whole tragic process must flow from an inward state of being, not from historical conditions. Conflict and rebellion are largely internal affairs, as the solitary, superior soul of the hero is torn apart only to be gloriously restored to wholeness. There are those broad-minded critics for whom this is an intriguing new variant of the tragic tradition, and those more puristic souls for whom it is not tragedy at all.

In *Either/Or*, Søren Kierkegaard sees the hallmark of modern tragedy as the absolute self-responsibility (and thus absolute guilt) of a protagonist who stands or falls entirely by virtue of his own acts. One may contrast this with the ancient version of the art, with its intricate interplay of crime and innocence, self and Other, free agent and constraining circumstance.[49] In Kierkegaard's eyes, such tragic individualism is to be commended. It represents a gain on what has gone before. This is not the case for Hegel, however, who argues in his *Aesthetics* that modern tragedy individualises conflict in a way which reduces it to a purely external, accidental affair. The tragic hero of antiquity is a higher species of being, one who is raised above the average citizen and is subject to necessity in a special way. Such figures are, in Hegel's view, the medium of world-historical forces, but this cannot be said of the more richly psychologised characters of the modern tragic stage. Shakespeare's tragic art, for example, springs not from the rigorous unfolding of fate but from infelicitous circumstances which might always have been different. Reconciliation becomes a more inward, psychological affair, as it does for neo-Hegelian critics such as A.C. Bradley in his *Shakespearean Tragedy*. With the disappearance of the idea of destiny, routed by a modern sense of the random and contingent, the art of an Aeschylus or Sophocles is no longer possible. It is a prejudice Hegel shares with his philosophical adversary Friedrich Nietzsche, for whom modern tragedy ceased to be an art of the public sphere and instead has been individualised and driven inward. Nietzsche's hopes for the revival of a tragic culture turn on the renewal of that sphere in which the emergence of a shared mythology will play a vital role.

The death of tragedy can sometimes be code for the death of Greek tragedy. Some of those who identify the art with the theatre of Aeschylus, Sophocles and Euripides tend to announce its end when they encounter tragedies conceived in different historical circumstances. This is certainly the case with Thomas Rymer's *A Short View of Tragedy: Its Original Excellence and Corruption* (1693), as the title would suggest. It is as though one were to declare that poetry is dead because it is no longer invariably composed in heroic couplets, or that the Boeing is not an aircraft because it is not a Tiger Moth. We have been informed often enough that gods, myths, fate, high-born protagonists, a spirit of exaltation and a sense of the numinous are essential to tragedy, but we have not usually been told why. Perhaps the role of the Olympians in Greek tragedy is to demonstrate the stout-heartedness of those who challenge their malevolent schemes or bravely submit to the destiny they decree; but one can dramatise such virtues without a pantheon of morally disreputable deities to hand, and a good deal of later tragedy does precisely this.

Far from putting paid to tragedy, modernity may well have lent it a new lease of life. For one thing, it has immeasurably swollen the ranks of potential tragic protagonists. In a democratic age, anyone plucked from the street and placed in an intolerably tight spot is a possible candidate. As Rita Felski remarks, 'in this democratised vision of suffering, the soul of a bank clerk or a shop girl becomes a battleground on which momentous and incalculable forces play themselves out'.[50] Horace advises the poets not to allow the gods to speak in plebeian accents, and neither no doubt should tragic heroes, but when it comes to modern-day heroes we have set aside this piece of snobbery. From the Enlightenment onwards, we are confronted with the mind-shaking proposition (one long anticipated by Christianity) that men and women are to be valued simply on account of their membership of the human species, not because of their rank, character, gender or ethnic provenance.

In this sense, it is difference that can be reactionary, not identity. Arthur Miller points out that psychoanalytic theory plays its part in this revolutionary creed, since the strategies of the unconscious are indifferent to social divisions.[51] One antique source of both comedy and tragedy is the fact that anyone can desire anyone else. Desire is no respecter of social distinctions, and the same is true of its Freudian terrible twin, death. Even so, the idea that anyone can be the subject of tragedy can carry a less positive implication. It may mean that tragedy is the only exceptional achievement which lies within the reach of ordinary people. It is this that Eugene O'Neill has in mind when he writes that 'The tragedy of Man is perhaps the only significant thing about him. . . . The individual life is made significant just by the struggle.'[52] The modern age is so morally bankrupt that a tragic end is the only value most of us can aspire to.

There are other reasons why modernity may facilitate tragedy rather than frustrate it. We are newly aware of the limits of reason, the frailty and self-opaqueness of the once sovereign human subject, its exposure to enigmatic forces beyond its control, the constraints placed on its agency and autonomy, its source in an anonymous Other which seems blankly indifferent to its well-being, the inevitable conflict of goods in a pluralistic culture, the complex density of a social order in which human damage can spread like typhoid. It is a condition not wholly remote from that of a small, tightly interwoven culture such as the Athens of the tragedians. In post-Freudian times, we, too, may find it possible to ask who is performing a certain action, even if the answer in our case is not Hera or Zeus, or whether there is not built into our behaviour some fatal hiatus between intention and effect. Bound together on a globalised planet, a sense of original sin – the knowledge that we, as guilty innocents, cannot move in this thick mesh of connections without unwittingly causing harm to someone, somewhere – stages a return. There is also the question of whether the planet will survive humanity's ultimate act of hubris, whether it takes the form of ecological disaster or nuclear devastation. Such is the nature of 'the power that a man summons against his own being when he turns his back on it', as Hegel puts it.[53] Besides, by breeding such Faustian aspirations, modernity risks witnessing their ignominious collapse. No historical period has unleashed human powers as abundantly as the modern era, and none is therefore more at risk of being mastered by the forces it unchains. As Max Weber remarks, 'The multitude of ancient gods, disenchanted and therefore in the form of impersonal forces, are climbing out of their graves, striving for power over our lives and resuming their eternal struggle with one another.'[54]

For all its insensitivity to human suffering, there is something to be said for the apparently perverse claim that tragedy is an affirmative mode, once it has been shorn of a whole set of dubious assumptions: that this is because it portrays the triumph of the indomitable human spirit, that to confront adversity is invariably to be tempered and chastened, that only at such an extreme is the stuff of humanity laid bare, or that the profile of a providential order may be visible through what may seem on the face of it pure misfortune. These are not the most convincing ways in which tragedy can inspire its audience. It is rather that the spectacle of those who are in mortal danger or atrocious pain can renew our sense of the value of the humanity which is under siege. Even so, what the philosophers of tragedy generally fail to add is that there are other, equally fruitful ways of recalling what we cherish about human beings – that we do not appreciate their worth only by watching them die.

There are those such as Jacques Lacan and Slavoj Žižek for whom the Gulag and Holocaust cannot be described as tragic, since the horror they reveal runs so deep that it cannot be sublimated into tragic dignity.[55] To describe the stricken inmates of the Nazi camps as tragic, Žižek asserts, is a moral obscenity. It is as though the mere act of assigning a meaning to such outrages is a gesture of betrayal. But the meaningless is the absurd, and the Gulag and Holocaust were certainly not that. To claim that they make a kind of sense is not thereby to invest them with value. The intelligible is not the same as the morally acceptable. There are those who fear that to speak coherently of the death camps is to collude with the repressive forms of reason that helped to create them. Yet rationality also played a key role in bringing these enormities to an end. In any case, it is not as if we face a choice between the utterly senseless on the one hand and the luminously meaningful on the other.

One does not need to embrace absurdity in order to undercut some grand scheme of significance, even though there can be an element of the ludicrous in the most exalted of tragedies. Ancient Greek tragedy is aware that there is that which transcends our sense-making, but this is not to say that human atrocities defeat all reasoning. Thomas Aquinas holds that when we speak of God we do not know what we are talking about, but he fills a large number of volumes with such talk even so. For Freud, non-meaning lies at the root of meaning, but this is no reason to abandon signification as a bad job.

In any case, *pace* Žižek, there is no need for an event to involve dignity or nobility in order for it to qualify as tragic. It is necessary, to be sure, for it to involve a sense of value, but this need not be manifest in some grandeur of spirit in the figures we see on stage. It may be we, the audience, who act as the custodians of their humanity when they themselves feel it slipping away from them. Eugene O'Neill claims that tragedy must have a 'transfiguring nobility' about it,[56] but he fails to note this distinction between the experience of the characters and that of the audience. The inmates of Belsen or Buchenwald did not have to die hallowed by their sufferings, or with a brave resignation to their fate, or conscious of themselves as world-historical figures, or exulting in the thought that, though they themselves might perish, the human spirit itself is invincible, in order to earn the title of tragic. They simply had to be men and women in an intolerable situation. The banal truth is that one does not need to do anything in particular to qualify as a tragic protagonist. One simply has to be a human being at the end of one's tether. One does not have to be virtuous, only virtuous enough not to deserve the wretchedness to which you are reduced. Tragedy, in Schopenhauerian phrase, is the fable of a great misfortune. It does not matter whether it occurs on- or off-stage, whether it is visited upon you by Zeus or happens through sheer accident,[57] whether the protagonist is a princess or a chauffeur, whether you engineer your own downfall or are cut down by others, whether the event results in reconciliation or a dead end, or whether it bears witness to a transcendent human spirit. By and large, it is the general public, faithful to these tenets, who use the word tragedy in the most productive way, and the theoreticians who generally fail to do so.[58]

Tragedy presents human beings in states of extremity, which is no doubt one reason why modernism, which is much preoccupied with what one might call the Room 101 of the human spirit, is so hospitable to the form. As J.M. Coetzee remarks in *Waiting for the Barbarians*, 'the last truth is told only in the last extremity'. It is the torturer's view of humanity, one which assumes that truth and everyday life are antithetical. On this view, the tragic protagonist is pitched into a situation which causes his routine illusions and run-of-the-mill compromises to fall from him like so many rags, as he is brought eyeball to eyeball with the truth of his identity. As we shall see in a later chapter, Arthur Miller's Willy Loman is a mixed specimen in this respect. Willy clings to his false consciousness to the end; yet, in refusing to back down from this bogus identity, he also refuses to give up on his demand for recognition, one which a corrupt society is unable to satisfy. It is this terrifying tenacity, at once courageous and deluded, which drives him into solitude and death.

In this sense, Loman displays an admirable yet alarming intransigence, one which stalks the tragic stage as early as Sophocles' stiff-necked, curmudgeonly, magnificently unyielding protagonists. There is a tradition of tragic figures who are driven by some inner compulsion to stay loyal to a commitment which engulfs the whole of their being and who would prefer to be dragged to their death rather than give way on a desire which they prize more than existence itself. It is this which Jacques Lacan names the desire of the Real, a form of longing in which *Eros* and *Thanatos* are closely interwoven.[59] Nowhere is this refusal more obvious than in the Lacanian reading of Sophocles' *Antigone*, a figure who, in *The Ethics of Psychoanalysis*, Lacan regards as inhabiting some transcendent realm beyond reason, ethics and signification, an enigmatic avatar of the Absolute who takes her stand on the extreme edge of the symbolic order and cannot support being subject to its law. Since death also lurks on that border, it is not surprising that it and the heroine should find themselves on such intimate terms.[60]

True to this reading of the play, Slavoj Žižek claims that Antigone represents an 'unconditional fidelity to the Otherness of the Thing that disrupts the entire social edifice'.[61] In the confrontation between Creon and Antigone, Žižek comments, there is 'no dialogue, no attempt (on the part of Antigone) to convince Creon of the good reasons for her acts through rational arguments, just blind insistence on her rights'.[62] We are invited to admire a character who is deaf to reason, disdainful of human society, arrogantly inflexible in her supreme self-belief, enraptured by the idea of death, loftily dismissive of the minor but creditable virtue of prudence and with no very firm grasp of her own motivation. Her act of defying Creon is one of pure refusal and rebellion, a 'miraculous' event striking at the foundations of the social order. If this is so, then it is not clear why she is presented by the play as acting in obedience to time-honoured obligation and the will of the gods.

It is striking how this idealised figure, who at times sails embarrassingly close to the adolescent pseudo-existentialist of Jean Anouilh's version of Sophocles' play, is so exactly in line with the spiritually elitist reading of tragedy we have considered already. The Lacanian interpretation of *Antigone* is a legatee of this conservative lineage, while lending it an apparently radical twist. Lacan's high-toned disdain for everyday life is a familiar feature of leftist French thought, with its devotion to some pure act, higher truth, adamant refusal, gratuitous gesture, purifying violence, absolute rebellion or glamorous cult of authenticity. A reckless patrician distaste for prudence, equivalence and calculation is preferable to the counting-house mentality of the petty bourgeoisie. The aesthetic splendour of a pure act of revolt counts for more than commonplace acts of compassion. In a politics of perpetual revolt, one more bohemian than Bolshevik, the mad, violent, evil and monstrous subvert the dreary orthodoxies of suburban society.

Yet not all orthodoxies are pernicious, nor all subversions revolutionary. Social orthodoxy currently includes the protection of ethnic minorities from abuse and the right of working men and women to withdraw their labour. In *The Parallax View*, Slavoj Žižek adopts Kierkegaard's elitist distinction between the routinely ethical and the authentically religious.[63] Yet the scandal of the Christian Gospel is that God is most fundamentally present not in cult, ritual or inward experience but in the act of visiting the sick and feeding the hungry. The idea of the common life, loftily denigrated by so much theory of tragedy, was actually invented by Christianity, which is in some respects a form of anti-religion.[64] The ethical is simply how religious faith is lived out in everyday practice. For those who find a touch of bathos in this view, however, ethics is a domain reserved for the spiritual plebeians of this world, while the aristocrats of the inner life move in a sphere beyond good and evil.

If the eternal rebel loiters on the brink of the symbolic order with little but contempt for it in his heart, so does the terrorist. Antigone's challenge to an unjust authority may be a 'monstrous' act, at least from the standpoint of social convention, but blowing the heads off small children fits that description rather more exactly. Stiff-necked patriarchs such as Creon offer an easy enough target for the Antigones of this world, but what if such refuseniks were to find themselves up against a socialist–feminist order? Would their champions still be so eager to honour their act of rejection? The opposition between the rebel and the political order is purely formalistic. It obscures the question of what form of revolt is at stake, against what type of sovereignty. There are precious forms of authority and infantile acts of dissent.

What this version of Antigone has to offer is really a form of left elitism. In some ways it is a radical version of Steinerism, right down to the question of the death of tragedy. Quoting Hegel's famous dictum that no man is a hero to his valet, Žižek complains that in the modern age 'all dignified higher stances are reduced to lower motivations'.[65] Modernity has diminished the capacity for sublimity. For him, as for the Nietzsche of *Untimely Meditations*, we are condemned to exist in a world without heroes, a prospect which gladdened the heart of Bertolt Brecht. What Žižek terms ethical violence – a situation in which, since moral standpoints are mutually incommensurable, we have to fight it out rather than strive for agreement – has yielded ground to a despicable consensualism. In a Nietzschean vein, life itself is Will to Power, a matter of struggle and contention. We must accordingly break through our Habermasian (or Apollonian) illusions of rationality by mustering the spiritual vigour we need to stare the Real (or Dionysian) in the face.[66]

Yet it is not true, as the conservative account of tragedy (including its Lacanian version) assumes, that extremity and the common life are always at loggerheads. The fact that everything carries on as normal, remarks Walter Benjamin, *is* the crisis.[67] George Eliot speaks in *Middlemarch* of 'that element of tragedy which lies in the very fact of frequency', meaning those states of quiet desperation which are generally too persistent for us to treat with the sensitivity they demand. In her own society, they were usually the experience of women. 'If we had a keen vision and feeling of all ordinary human life,' Eliot remarks, 'it would be like hearing the grass grow and the squirrel's heart beat, and we should die of that roar which lies on the other side of silence. As it is, the quickest of us walk about well wadded with stupidity.' Such well-wadded insulation from pain would certainly seem the case with some traditional theorists of tragedy.

2

INCEST AND ARITHMETIC

It has long been apparent that *Oedipus Tyrannus* has an arithmetical subtext.[1] Laius, Oedipus's father, is killed at a place where three roads meet; the Sphinx whom Oedipus outsmarts is a compound of different creatures; and the riddle with which it terrorises the local population not only involves numbers but rolls three phases of human existence into one question. The play contains a famously unresolved puzzle over whether Laius was slain by one or several assailants.[2] If it was several, then Oedipus cannot be guilty of parricide; but it is possible that we are guilty whether we have done anything or not, or that we can never know for sure whether we have done anything or not. As Maurice Merleau-Ponty comments, 'The whole of Greek tragedy assumes this idea of an essential contingency through which we are all guilty and innocent because we do not know what we are doing.'[3]

Oedipus, who testily insists that one is not more than one, is precisely this himself, as both son and husband, father and brother, criminal and lawgiver, king and beggar man, native and stranger, poison and cure, man and monster, guilty and innocent, blind and perspicacious, holy and cursed, swift of mind and slow of foot, solver of riddles and indecipherable enigma.[4] He is a man brilliantly proficient at bringing himself to nothing. As one critic remarks, he exhibits 'an unstable arithmetic of the self'.[5] One can never be quite sure how many one is. Counting is not quite the straightforward exercise it seems, as the discrepancy over how many individuals murdered Laius would suggest. All men and women are the offspring of innumerable ancestors, composed of so many finely inter-woven strands that they are effectively illegible texts. It is clear in any case from Sophocles' drama that, *pace* postmodernism, not all plurality is benign, not all hybridity angelic and not all insistence on identity enlightened.

As more than one, Oedipus is no more than anyone, since all individuals, if only by virtue of being both subjects and objects, are necessarily non-self-identical. Moreover, to occupy a place in the symbolic order is to play a whole series of roles simultaneously (mother, aunt, cousin, sister and so on), as the bumptious Bottom seeks to do in *A Midsummer Night's Dream*. In any case, there is always a degree of playacting in being oneself. *Oedipus Tyrannus* may be, among other things, a play about role-playing, but as a piece of theatre it is also a material example of such doubling – of an instability of self-hood which accounts, among other reasons, for Plato's frosty attitude to dramatic performance in the *Republic*. The theatre also deals in doubling in the sense of reflecting the *polis* back to itself, in a way which, as we have seen, can both challenge and confirm its sense of identity. If the audience can see itself in an estranging light, one which has the power to unsettle its conventional self-understanding, it can also struggle to assimilate this dangerous knowledge and come to terms with it.

Oedipus, like the rest of humankind, is also split between his perception of himself and that version of his identity which is in the custodianship of the Other. What he is from that standpoint (an incestuous parricide) is not what he is for himself, and the true meaning of his unwittingly ambiguous speech, as with that of any human utterance, is determined by its location in the Other (the whole field of language, kinship and social relations), not primarily by his conscious intentions. The truth of the ego does not coincide with the truth of the subject. Something alien acts and speaks in this proudly self-determining figure, persisting as a riddling subtext within his speech, in fact even within his name, decentring his imaginary identity and finally driving him to his death.

The discrepancy between how Oedipus speaks and how he is spoken reveals humanity itself to be irony incarnate. It is part of that irony that what sets up the conscious subject in the first place – the Other or social unconscious – is bound to elude its knowledge, since there is no viewpoint from which one might grasp it as a whole, no other of the Other. In any case, the ego comes into being through the act of thrusting into oblivion much of what goes into its making, so that it belongs to one's identity that one can never be entirely self-identical. Psychoanalytically speaking, one can never simply be one, since it is a primordial splitting which brings the subject into being in the first place. When Oedipus finally encounters his true self, it will confront him as a stranger. He is never more lost to himself than when he comes face to face with the truth of who he is. The crisis of recognition is also the moment of blindness. Knowledge illuminates, but with a dazzle that puts out your eyes. When the truth stands unveiled, it turns out to be the truth of ignorance and delusion.

As ruler, Oedipus is already many-in-one, bearing responsibility for the whole community on his shoulders. 'My heart bears the weight of my own, and yours and all my people's sorrows,' he tells the Priest. In the peculiar arithmetic of incest, each individual is also several-in-one. The incest taboo states that two into one won't go, but sexuality refuses to conform to such strictures.[6] In regular sexual reproduction, $1 + 1 = 1$, leaving aside cases of multiple offspring, but what is the formula for an act of sexual reproduction in which the female partner conflates four roles, being wife and mother to her husband and mother-cum-grandmother of their children; the male partner does likewise, being both son and husband of the woman and father and brother of their children; and the child is daughter, sister and granddaughter together? Incest is thus a particularly arresting case of irony, in which a thing is both itself and something else, and irony of one kind or another permeates every fibre of Sophocles' masterpiece.

Yet we have seen already that for a thing to be both itself and something else – for a woman, for example, to be at the same time mother, cousin, aunt and daughter – is a constitutive feature of the symbolic order; so that whatever is amiss with incest, it cannot be sheer multiplicity. The transgression of boundaries is routine business. Jocasta, trying to take the steam out of a bad situation, remarks that many a man has dreamed of sleeping with his mother. Besides, for the kinship system to operate effectively, incest must be a perpetual possibility. If roles must be flexible enough to be combined, then illicit permutations are likely to crop up from time to time. In this sense, the deviant is a condition of the normative – rather as civilised society, like Oedipus himself with his injured foot, emerges from violent origins. The desire which generates the symbolic order in the first place can always override the precepts which hold it in place.

The monster is traditionally a creature who, like the Sphinx, elides distinctions, garbles differences and amalgamates features which ought properly to be distinct. As Richard McCabe remarks with regard to the 'loss or uncertainty of identity' implied in incest, 'the confounding of traditional kinship vocabulary entails a regression to Babel, a confounding of intelligible values'.[7] In one of the classic understatements of the modern age, Roland Barthes describes it as a 'surprise of vocabulary'.[8] The monster is a thing which can return no determinate answer to the question 'What is that?', any more than humanity itself is capable of doing. In this sense, Oedipus and the Sphinx are mirror images as well as antagonists. If 'humanity' is the answer to the Sphinx's riddle, then Oedipus himself, as a spokesman for the species, is acknowledging its monstrous hybridity, and thus its affinity with the Sphinx, at the very moment that his agility of mind demonstrates his superiority to it.

Oedipus himself is the answer to the riddle, just as he himself is the outlaw he is pursuing. There is something mildly comic about this self-referential situation, with its hint of pointlessly chasing one's own tail. It mirrors the darker comedy of incest, which is the subject of some tolerably good jokes. No doubt such jesting is a defence against a mode of sexuality which shakes the mind to its roots, as a character in Iris Murdoch's novel *A Severed Head* remarks. But incestuous relations also display something of the incongruity that is a staple part of humour. Oedipus's comments on his own polluted condition – 'bridegroom son', 'begetter of brother-sons', 'breeding where I was bred' and the like – sound like grisly shafts of wit. It is a vein of *comédie noire* evident in the American satirist Tom Lehrer's song about Sophocles' hero:

'He loved his mother like no other, / His daughter was his sister and his son was his brother.' The Sphinx's riddle, rather similarly, borders on the kind of teaser one might find in a Christmas cracker. Incest is a form of excessive economy, portrayed here in a play which is a miracle of compactness itself, and in the case of jokes such economy allows us to save on psychical energy, which is then released in the form of laughter.

The monstrous and the incestuous both involve a confusion of categories. Yet if all occupants of the symbolic order are in any case hybrid, why should incest be singled out as an abomination? One reason is that it poses a threat to the *polis*. Without exogamous relationships, *Eros*, builder of cities, remains locked within the domestic sphere. As Franco Moretti remarks, 'Incest is that form of desire which makes impossible the matrimonial exchange that, in a society in which power is still connected with physical persons, reinforces and perpetuates the network of wealth.'[9] It is an anti-social passion, divorcing desire from settled social forms and thus risking the implosion of the symbolic order, along with the entire universe of meaning it sustains. As a garbling of that meaning, incest is a species of non-sense or absurdity, and thus much like a riddle.

So it is that one must encounter a stranger in the marriage bed if one is not, like Oedipus, to end up as a stranger to oneself. Part of the point of the incest taboo is to turn you outwards from the imaginary realm – which is to say from relationships involving identity, resemblance and mutual mirroring – to the terrain of the Other. The family is a place of emotional intimacy, unlike the political state; but it must also help to sustain the state (it is, for example, the place where labour power is reproduced), and thus cannot shut you off from it. The Imaginary must not be allowed to ride roughshod over the Symbolic. The ancient Greeks were scrupulous in their distinction between domestic affections, or love of one's kin, and an erotic attachment to strangers or non-kinsfolk. It is this opposition that incest undermines. It also betrays the fact that sexuality, in Eric Santner's words, 'is inherently perverse, inherently in excess of its teleological function (the reproduction of the family qua basic economic unit)'.[10] And if sexuality itself is perverse, then it is incest, not the domestic unit, which is the appropriate image of it.

Like *Oedipus Tyrannus*, the *Oresteia* and *Antigone* also concern a quarrel between the domestic and political domains. If *Antigone* turns on a confrontation between family and state, *Oedipus Tyrannus* does the same rather less starkly. Antigone's name may suggest that she stands opposed to the order of sexual reproduction, which is certainly the case with incest. It is the unmaking of that order not only because it can result in disabled offspring (the malformed Sphinx is itself is the product of incest), or because an awareness of this may prevent sexual reproduction altogether, but because it is transmissible down the generations in a parody of the normal line of inheritance.

Were Antigone to bear children herself, they would have an uncle for a grandfather. There can even be a double incest, as in Thomas Mann's novel *The Holy Sinner*, in which a child of incest then marries his own mother. It is to prevent man handing on misery to man, then, that the deadly line of descent must be cut off.

Incest, at least when it comes to illicit relations between parents and children, also threatens to put paid to history by eliding different generations. It is a kind of false equation, levelling parents with their own children. The Sphinx's riddle also merges distinct generations, yoking together infancy, adulthood and old age. The Oedipus who solves the puzzle is himself an example of it, as child of his wife, husband to her and older man (father) simultaneously. This hostility to narrative is why incestuous couples such as Giovanni and Anabella in John Ford's *'Tis Pity She's a Whore* seem to occupy a timeless sphere of their own, indifferent to lineage and reproduction. The same is true of the intense affinity between Heathcliff and Catherine in *Wuthering Heights*, who may be brother and sister. To deny temporality is also to disavow death, as in the love-relationship of Shakespeare's Antony and Cleopatra. That death is prefigured for the male subject in the castrating cut which severs him from the mother's body; but it can be avoided by clinging to the maternal flesh and refusing such a division. Yet, since this severance is also the opening up of difference, and thus of language and writing, literary works about incest are testimony to the fact that our expulsion from the happy garden has always already happened. Time, narrative and desire are all dependent on the disastrous, delightful event of the Fall (*felix culpa*, as it is traditionally known), which is to say on the moment when we relinquish the mother's body and exchange this felicity for a precarious degree of autonomy. Only by repressing this primordial trauma is it possible to carve a history for oneself. Even then, however, its baneful effects can never be wholly effaced, any more than Oedipus will ever cease to limp. The wounded foot, sign of the place where he has been torn by violence from the earth/mother, will not be made whole.

Oedipus is *tyrannus*, which is to say one who comes to power other than by lineal succession – though in a superbly ironic touch he turns out, as Laius's son, to be the legitimate heir after all. His discovery of his criminality is also the revelation of his legitimacy. It is appropriate, however, that the king should be an outsider, a blow-in from Corinth, a son of Thebes who considers himself an alien in the city, since the ruler is invested with an authority which sets him above the social order, and thus in a sense outside it. In this, he resembles the beggar or outlaw who is evicted from the human community. As a lone figure representing the multitude, the king's status as both one and many makes him akin to the monster. Monsters and monarchs are both freakish creatures. In the arithmetic of humanity, men and women are more than beasts but less than gods. The problem is that they constitute a contradictory compound of the two, rather than occupying some determinate middle ground between them; and this is also true of those who commit incest. It is possible to be god, man and monster in one, an unholy trinity of which Oedipus himself will end up as an example.

If Oedipus is not sovereign by lineal succession, neither does his career conform to a linear logic. Throughout the play, he moves not forwards but backwards, as the past invades the present to confound the future. One can be hobbled by the past – literally so in the case of King Swollen Foot. If literary plot depends upon temporal succession, then incest threatens to be the ruin of it, even if in this play it forms the subject of one of the shapeliest plots of world literature. If incest turns its back on progress and procreation, so does *Thanatos*, or the death drive, which is one way in which the two are linked. From *Oedipus Tyrannus* to *A View from the Bridge*, incestuous desire brings men and women to their doom. It is the monster lurking at the heart of the symbolic order which, like the Sphinx, confounds all carefully calibrated distinctions and brings death and devastation in its wake. If this rough beast lurks in the borderlands of the social order, so, too, does death, which also levels distinctions and lays bare their arbitrary nature. In its obliteration of difference, as well as in its obscene enjoyment, incest has something of the Real or Dionysian about it. The enjoyment in question springs from gaining access to that most impossible of all objects, the body of the mother. It is this too-intimate thing which must be kept at bay if our Apollonian illusions are to be preserved, our narratives recounted and our symbolic fictions, which include the theatre itself, are to function smoothly. One can sustain one's identity only through a redemptive blindness to the noumenal, unclean, traumatic thing which lies at the core of one's being.

Knowledge of incest is knowledge of the unnatural, but there is a sense in which knowledge is unnatural anyway. It involves trying to stand outside the Nature to which we belong and view it through objectifying eyes. Its attempt to penetrate the world's inner stuff is traditionally associated with criminality. Since Nature is traditionally seen as the mother of humanity, delving into its secret places is an incestuous business. Only by unnatural acts, claims Friedrich Nietzsche in *The Birth of Tragedy*, can Nature be forced to yield up its secrets. Wisdom is a crime against Nature, he declares, gleefully equating knowledge with rape. Or, as Freud was later to remark, 'without criminality there is no achievement'.[11]

Humanity is always either too estranged from the world or too intimate with it – either standing outside it like a king, outlaw or Olympian, or too caught up in its toils to be able to see it for what it is. There is an epistemological question implicit in Sophocles' play: what distance must one establish from an object in order to have genuine knowledge of it? This is a particular problem when it comes to knowing oneself. Incest may be unnatural, but so, rather less sensationally, is self-knowledge. It is this that Oedipus is in pursuit of, but achieving it would seem to demand almost as unnatural a doubling as being son and husband to the same woman. How can one be both subject and object of one's inquiry, as Oedipus is both detective and law-breaker? Is it not like trying to leap on your own shadow, or haul yourself up by your own boot-straps? To know yourself is to be self-identical, but it also involves splitting yourself in two, turning yourself into an object and thus implicitly denying one's subjectivity in the very act of exercising it. As with incest, it is a question of two-in-one. Besides, if the self is changed by the act of knowing it, how can one ever catch up with oneself?

Against this self-division one can set a dream of autonomy – the fiction of some total self-presence or absolute self-authoring which would necessarily include being sovereign over one's own origin. One's birth, after all, is the very paradigm of fate – not only because we do not get to choose it, rather as we do not get to choose our bodies, but because of its influence on the rest of one's existence. It is this dependence that the double act of incest and parricide aims to eliminate, disposing of one's progenitors by killing one's father and turning one's mother into a wife. One is now as self-made as the *tyrannus*, who relies on no royal pedigree to legitimate his rule but who wrests the prize of kingship simply by virtue of his talents. Yet how is to be self-made not to be a monster? In antiquity, a monster could mean a creature cut off from all kinship as well as some frightfully disfigured beast, so that Oedipus is monstrous in at least two meanings of the term. To be utterly self-determining, and thus to be on too familiar terms with oneself, involves repudiating the networks of kinship and social relations by which the self is constituted; and this in turn means becoming a stranger to oneself. Oedipus's desire is to be like Shakespeare's Coriolanus, who behaves 'As if a man were author of himself / And knew no other kin' (Act 5, sc. 3).

Incest, too, involves an interplay of strangeness and intimacy. In approaching too close to the sources of one's being, one becomes a mystery to oneself, since men and women are who they are by virtue of their relationships, and relationship demands distance. The boundaries between difference and identity, otherness and affinity, begin to blur. The incestuous son re-enters his mother's womb, vanishing into his own origin and thus ending up lost to himself. Yet incest also reflects our everyday condition. In the tangle of human actions, the constitutive strands of which can never be fully unravelled, we are all both aliens and associates, unwittingly allied with those who appear outsiders. The stranger at the crossroads is never entirely foreign. Even the most private of our actions are derived from the anonymous Other, so that (for example) to declare one's love means pronouncing phrases which belong to no one and which are shop-soiled by countless previous uses.

The sources of human action are diverse and obscure. 'Is this act mine or not?' is not an absurd inquiry as 'Is this pain mine or not?' would be. It is not always easy to say where one agent ends and another begins. Our most trifling acts can spawn momentous consequences over which we have no control. Eric Auerbach rightly understands the Christian doctrine of original sin as 'the inextricable fabric of heredity, historical situation, individual temperament, and the consequences of our own actions, in which we are everlastingly involved'.[12] It is all this that Oedipus, gripped by a fantasy of self-fashioning, must learn to his cost. Indeed, so implacable is this fantasy that he must be confronted with a frightful parody of human interdependence, in the form of incest, for its truth to be brought home to him.

In the end, the arithmetical calculation which counts most is not the recognition that one is more than one, but that zero is more than zero. Only when Oedipus is brought to nothing can he become something – and the difference between something and nothing, as the doctrine of Creation would suggest, is the most fundamental difference of all. 'Am I made man in the hour that I cease to be?,' he asks in *Oedipus at Colonus*. It is not true, as Lear warns Cordelia, that nothing can come of nothing. That play, too, has an arithmetical subtext, ringing the changes on more, less, something, superfluity, all and nothing. Oedipus ends up as a mere cipher, a beggarly self-exile; yet only when he is blind will he grasp the truth, only when he is stripped of his humanity will he be genuinely human, only when he is destitute will he be raised up. In becoming less than his previous self, he succeeds in becoming more. Indeed, in his miraculous transfiguration at the end of *Oedipus at Colonus* nothing will become not merely something, but all – and that in a quite different sense from the omnipotent sway of the sovereign, a persona he has now cast off. In this sense, Sophocles' hero ends up by defeating all calculability, as indeed does *Oedipus Tyrannus* itself. At its centre, as we have seen, lies a puzzle over numbers – how many bandits killed Laius? – which it allows to go unresolved. This beautifully precise piece of art contains an anomaly or indeterminacy at its heart, and as such is true to the nature of humanity itself.

3

TRAGIC TRANSITIONS

All historical periods are times of transition, salvaging something from the past while looking to the future. Raymond Williams speaks in *Marxism and Literature* of how all societies are made up of the residual, the dominant and the emergent;[1] but one must grasp this model dynamically, since the dominant may be about to become residual, the emergent may be moving into the ascendant and the new may recapitulate the old. There are times, however, when consciousness of this change is keener than usual – when an age may actually feel itself in middle march or *medias res*, shaped by what lies behind it yet driven on by what is still to come, tugged by the tidal influence of both eras and anxiously or excitedly aware of its own experience as open-ended. There are periods such as the late eighteenth or early twentieth centuries in which the ground can be felt shifting beneath one's feet, as various seismic rumblings announce the arrival of some apocalyptic rough beast.

It is a familiar claim that these liminal states are the periods of major tragedy. It is true that tragedy of some sort happens all the time. When it breaks out on an epic scale, however, it is usually at times when one way of life collides with another, or when a traditional world-view, while still retaining a degree of authority, is confronted by forces it cannot easily accommodate. The present finds itself locked in combat with a past which is dying but cannot be despatched. It is not just that an older civilisation is breaking up, but that it becomes palpable in its very passing, rather as the intolerable burden of Jean Racine's God is felt most in his absence. 'Tragedy,' remarks Albert Camus, 'is born in the West each time that the pendulum of civilisation is halfway between a sacred society and a society build around humanity.'[2]

Don Quixote, writes Claudio Magris, 'is an epic of disenchantment that preserves, at least at first, deep echoes of epic poetry in the lucid new medium of prose'.[3] In fact, one might see the novel in general as a transitional form, one which recycles sacred, mythical, romantic or supernatural materials for secular ends. The fable or folk tale becomes a full-blown realist narrative. Yet the novel is sufficiently at ease with its historical moment not to feel the backward pull of these pre-modern worlds as poignantly as some tragedy does. As Georg Lukács argues in *Theory of the Novel*, the novel is a genre for which the idea of immanent meaning is steadily disintegrating, while men and women pick among the rubble to fashion a less sacralised sense of daily existence. They do so, however, with a growing assurance that for all practical purposes they can dispense with the mythical or supernatural, which now tend to crop up mainly when an author feels the need for some quasi-magical device to clear up a problem which cannot be resolved in realist terms. If the novel is a transitional form, it is not so much because it labours under the burden of the past while turning its face to the future, but because it is the product of a modernity which is itself in perpetual flux.

There is plenty of tragic art in which men and women strive to shape their own future only to find themselves thwarted by the remnants of an older dispensation. The period in which Greek tragedy was established was one of spectacular social and political turbulence, with internecine struggles between various aristocratic factions, growing popular resentment of the ruling class and the rise of popular tyrants. All this was eventually to give birth to a more public, impersonal, participatory brand of politics, in a community based less on kinship and custom than on common conventions.[4] Charles Segal sees *Oedipus Tyrannus* as a document of the fifth-century Athenian Enlightenment, with its shift from mythical and symbolic to more abstract and discursive thought.[5] Blair Hoxby argues that if Greek tragedy was such a short-lived cultural formation, it was because 'it could flourish only during the moment of cultural transition when religious habits of thought were on the wane but still possessed a measure of force and when legal concepts of responsibility were current but not yet unassailable'.[6] Jean-Pierre Vernant and Pierre Vidal-Naquet point out that the tragic hero generally hails from an earlier mythological era, but can now be distanced and critically appraised.[7] It is thus that the hero encounters the Chorus, who as ordinary members of the *polis* occupy the civic rather than mythological sphere, moving in a different dimension from the legendary figures with whom they enter into dialogue.

Tragedy, then, begins when myth is contemplated from the standpoint of the *polis* – though, in a two-way movement, such myths can also highlight the limits of the rationality which examines them. Heroic and religious values become subject to the legal, ethical and political judgements of the city state, which needs to break with the mythological past in order to lay the ground for its own authority. However deeply the theatre of Dionysus remains indebted to this past, tragedy is in this sense an innovative affair. In *The Origin of German Tragic Drama*, Walter Benjamin sees Greek tragedy as a matter of myth, while the German *Trauerspiel* with which his book deals is a question of history; but he also points out that the Greek tragedians rework their mythological materials in a way that brings the heroic events of antiquity to bear on contemporary issues. Tragic art for Benjamin thus straddles both past and present. We shall see later how in his view it also anticipates the future.

'The institution of tragedy,' writes Simon Goldhill, 'is a machine to turn epic myth into the myths of the *polis*.'[8] It is, he adds, 'the staged display of practical reason'.[9] The plots of these works deal largely with fable and legend, yet, as realist treatments of what are often non-realist materials, they do so in terms of rational discourse and critical debate. Whereas epic reports on the past as past, Goldhill points out, tragedy brings that past alive again in the present, and in combining the two is transitional in its very form. Through the power of mimesis, the historically remote can be brought palpably before our eyes. To fictionalise is also to detach events from their original context in order to foster more wide-ranging reflections on their meaning, so that, in this sense, too, the stuff of an imaginary past encounters the forensic spirit of the modern.

Even so, though men and women can now be objects of critical reflection, they have not yet evolved into autonomous Kantian subjects. In the riddle of the Sphinx, human beings stand on their own two feet, but only in a brief interlude between crawling and hobbling. We enjoy a degree of self-mastery, but only within a deeper context of dependence. It is from this double determination – this tension between the self as the source of its own actions and the sibylline Other that speaks and acts through it – that a good deal of tragic conflict springs. 'In tragedy,' remarks Joshua Billings, 'the words of the gods are always riddles, and the protagonists' knowledge is never free from ignorance.'[10] It is the gradual emergence of truth from such partial knowledge that for Hegel marks the tragic art of antiquity. We have seen already that the meaning of one's action for the Other – its location within the whole field of power, inheritance, kinship, signification, the gods – may fail to coincide with its meaning for oneself, so that the true significance of your conduct slips from your grasp and may recoil on you later in alien form. As Jean-Pierre Vernant and Pierre Vidal-Naquet remark, 'the only authentic truth in Oedipus's words is what he says without meaning and understanding it'.[11] One can never entirely call one's words or actions one's own. As August Strindberg's play *The Father* is aware, there is no starker image of this self-estrangement than paternity, since one's child is the fruit of a past act which now leads a life of its own, and in any case may not be yours in the first place.

One must therefore calculate one's actions prudently, weaving one's path through a minefield of inscrutable powers and contending forces. Rather, as there can be no final metalanguage, since one would need another language in which to explicate it, so, as we have seen, there can be no other to the Other – no viewpoint from which you might grasp it as a whole. It is not a unified domain, any more than the squabbling deities of Mount Olympus constitute a single sovereignty. It is from the Other that one receives oneself back as a seemingly self-motivating agent; but this is bound to fall outside the dominion of the mind, since it is what constitutes us as cognitive subjects in the first place.

Oedipus, with his vigour of intellect, pride in his own powers and rather too bullish trust in the human capacity for knowledge, can be taken as typifying something of the critical spirit of enlightened Athenian humanism. Yet the keenness of the mind can be at odds with the finitude of the flesh, and the humanist injunction to know oneself can run up against an impenetrable otherness, whether one gives it the name of fate, the gods, the mystery of origins or the occult foundations of the self. 'When man decides, like Oedipus, to carry the inquiry into what he is as far as it can go,' write Vernant and Vidal-Naquet, 'he discovers himself to be enigmatic, without consistency, without any domain of his own or any fixed point of attachment, with no defined essence, oscillating between being the equal of the gods and being the equal of nothing at all.'[12] As such, this beggarly king is both a model of enlightenment and an instrument of its critique. He is knowledge at the end of its tether. The name Oedipus might mean among other things 'know-foot', but this is a form of knowledge beyond our power. The injured foot, as we have seen, marks the place where we are torn from the earth, the wound of autonomous selfhood which allows us to stand precariously by ourselves; but the foot itself is where we are anchored to the earth, an earth which represents the impenetrable ground of our existence. This depth, like the mystery of one's individual origins, baffles all attempts at mastery by the mind. The crawling child of the Sphinx's riddle is close to the ground, and the old man's dependence on Nature is signified by the fact that he leans on the earth with a piece of wood hacked from it; but between infancy and old age the calculating head is at its furthest from the earth-bound feet, remote from the obscure place from which humanity emerges and to which it shall eventually return.

By returning the answer 'man' to the Sphinx's riddle, Oedipus, a solver of conundrums who is himself a conundrum, humanises the monstrous, as Jean-Joseph Goux points out.[13] Yet, in gentrifying monstrosity in this way, and thus seeking to disavow it, he also confesses that humanity is terrible beyond belief. The human is thus affirmed and undercut at a stroke. What Oedipus's austere arithmetic ('one is not more than one') is reluctant to acknowledge is the fact that humanity is constituted by an irreducible alterity. It is both flesh and spirit, rather as the Sphinx is both human and animal. The doubleness of human nature is disowned in the act of incest, as one usurps the father's role, becomes one's own progenitor and accordingly denies one's creaturely origins. One can now be pure spirit, no longer beholden to the flesh of others. To be in on the moment of one's own origin, to wipe one's pedigree clean, is the ultimate denial of dependency. In Hegel's view, Oedipus is thus the very prototype of the philosopher, since philosophy after Kant means slaying the symbolic father (tradition, conventional wisdom) in order to think and act for oneself. In this respect, blinding yourself is an ambiguous act. In one sense, it is part of the drive for self-sovereignty, which has been Oedipus's compulsion all along. Only suicide can outdo it. To kill oneself is to assume a godlike authority over one's existence. Yet in acting out his self-ignorance, the *coup de théâtre* by which Oedipus puts out his own eyes also brings him an awareness of the flesh and a reliance on others, thus opening the way to a new kind of self-understanding. As the blinded Gloucester remarks in *Lear*, 'I stumbled when I saw.'

In an age-old tragic rhythm, the self as subject can come into its own only on the basis of the self as object – as blinded, fragile, humbled and exposed. Genuine nobility of spirit consists in making one's finitude one's own. The Sphinx has a human head, but one incorporated into an animal body. Only by clinging to the vulnerable flesh can the mind avoid over-leaping itself and bringing itself to nothing. What is true in any case of human beings – that consciousness arises from their bodily interactions as infants – is converted from a fact to a value. We emerge into selfhood on the basis of the body – a lump of natural material which is both one's own and not one's own, the locus of subjectivity but in no sense a piece of property. It is the fruit of a narrative beyond our control, as well as being impersonal stuff we share in common. Humanity is also a doubled species in that it is both blessed and cursed, all and nothing, a wonder to behold and a ravaging beast, and so well-nigh impossible to bring into conceptual focus. As the Chorus of *Antigone* sings, humanity is both splendid and sinful – not simply mixed and many-sided, as a certain liberal wisdom would maintain, but contradiction incarnate, a riddle which resists all logic and eludes the reach of its own rationality. Tragedy, then, is a form of reason beyond all reason. It is a model of the dialectical knowledge of humanity.

To be a human body is to be an agent; but it is also to be passive and vulnerable, an object of history as well as a subject of it. The Sphinx is a devourer of raw flesh who tears off its victims' heads and, though Oedipus uses his own head to outsmart it, it, too, is metaphorically speaking severed, divorced by his cleverness from the wisdom of the body (a body which is itself a legacy from one's forebears), as well as from the network of pieties and obligations in which all human flesh is caught up. Since the Nature to which the body belongs is older than consciousness, the human animal is an inherently transitional creature, caught on the hop between flesh and spirit. Without reason we perish, as Pelasgus remarks in Aeschylus's *The Suppliants*; but reason does not go all the way down, and it is this lesson that the rationalism of an enlightened age must take to heart. 'Greek tragedy,' argues Bernard Williams, 'represents human beings as dealing sensibly, foolishly, sometimes catastrophically with a world which is only partially intelligible to human agency and is itself not necessarily well adjusted to ethical aspirations.'[14] It is a vision at its starkest in the drama of Euripides, with its sceptical, demystifying, chance-ridden universe, its scathing critique of war and of the insolence of power, its compassion for the dumped and disregarded, its anti-heroic realism and sober assessment of the limits of human reason. Yet, for all that there may be a dearth of rationality on Mount Olympus, the gods continue to intrude into human affairs. The *ancien régime* may be fractious and futile, but its power, however capricious, cannot be ignored.

In Aeschylus's *Oresteia*, the passage from mythology to politics, Nature to Culture, blood kinship to the civic sphere, raises among other things the question of hegemony – which is to say, of the relative proportions of coercion and consent essential for effective governance. The most prominent modern theorist of hegemony, Antonio Gramsci, sometimes uses the term to mean consensual rather than coercive power; but it can also signify a fusion of the two modes, which is what the *Oresteia* would appear to advocate as well.[15] There can be no simple polarity between the two in a well-ordered state. Not only must one resort to the means of coercion when consent has failed, but these means must themselves command general assent in order to achieve their ends. Brute force must be tempered by persuasion, but not to the point where its authority is eroded. Both principles, the one harsh and the other gentle, are contained in the nature of Zeus, in contrast to the God of Christianity, whose violence is nothing less than his ruthless, intolerable love. Rather as Edmund Burke's *Philosophical Enquiry into the*

Origin of our Ideas of the Sublime and Beautiful holds that the masculine Law, while cloaking itself in the seductive garments of a woman, must retain a certain phallic terror, so Aeschylus's Athene, while singing the praises of what she calls 'Holy Persuasion', admonishes the state not to banish from its armoury the weapon of fear, which may be brandished from time to time in the interests of civic order. Such terror must be preserved, but at a more civilised level – which is to say, in Hegelian terms, sublated or *aufgehoben.*

Power will truly flourish only when it succeeds in implanting itself in the affections of those it governs, but it must take care not to diminish itself in doing so. Intimidation remains essential, hard though it is to blend with affection. Those who use power with gentleness are to be admired, but not if they end up endangering the state. An excess of intimacy, as in the matter of incest, will merely spread havoc. 'There is no law in a city where there is no fear,' insists Menelaus in Sophocles' *Ajax*. The barbarous past must be incorporated into the urbane present, not disowned in an access of liberal enlightenment. This, to be sure, will take time, which is of the essence of hegemony. It is the passage of decades and centuries which converts sovereignty into a second nature, so that primordial crimes come to grow on us like old cronies and we come to desire the Law rather than simply tolerate it. Longevity is legitimacy. 'Power newly won is always harsh,' remarks Hephaestus in *Prometheus Bound*.

Intimidation and affection are rough equivalents of the sublime and the beautiful, and these must be yoked together in the practice of statecraft, as powers which threaten to lay waste to the *polis* are confronted, sublimated and turned outwards for its protection. It is in this way that armies are born. So it is that the loathsome Furies mutate into the Eumenides or Kindly Ones, becoming both sublime and beautiful, dreadful and benign. As resident aliens, they are at once frightful and familiar. In order to thrive, the *polis* must acknowledge the violence which brought it to birth and continues to lurk at its foundations, as the Eumenides are granted a dwelling place beneath the earth. The primal aggression they signify must be gentrified, a process that may involve a period of suffering. It is likely that, after his travails, Aeschylus's Prometheus would finally have been reconciled with a rather more congenial President of the Immortals; indeed, he himself assures the tormented Io that Zeus will finally come upon her 'not with terror, but with a gentle touch'.

Without such clemency, men and women will be locked in the windless antechamber of prehistory, caught up in the sterile cycles of slaughter and vengeance, unable to launch out on a truly historical narrative. They will be trapped in what William Golding's novel *Free Fall* calls 'the lethal line of descent', as actions spin out of their agents' control to breed unforeseen consequences, merging into an anonymous mesh in which individuals struggle as helplessly as Agamemnon in his deathly net. Trying to extricate yourself from this situation may simply sink you deeper into it. Revenge scuppers the possibility of narrative, folding the present back into the past and thus sabotaging the future. If it is the enemy of civilisation, it is not least because it arrests the temporal process by which such an order must evolve.

'The greatness of the Elizabethan age,' comments E.M.W. Tillyard, 'was that it contained so much of the new without bursting the noble form of the old order.'[16] There was in fact nothing conspicuously noble about the warring barons and colonial plunder of the Elizabethan order, whose conduct in Ireland was tantamount to genocide. Tillyard's anodyne image of containment suggests a peaceable accord between the old and the new, one which the tragic art of the period unmasks as largely spurious. In Jacobean tragedy in particular, the so-called noble order is wrecked beyond repair. 'It is a world that still thinks of itself as an organic whole,' writes Franco Moretti, 'but is ceasing – clamorously – to be so.'[17] For Johann Gottfried Herder, what marks Shakespeare's work is the sheer multiplicity of its life-forms, and only his individual genius can weld them into coherent shape.[18] Shakespeare's tragedies, Moretti maintains, are split between action and meaning, so that 'the axis of actions [the plot] is governed by one logic [i.e. will, power, passion] and the axis of values . . . by another, without either ever succeeding in overwhelming or expunging the other'.[19] 'In the main body of popular English drama,' writes Raymond Williams, 'it is clear that elements of an older tradition are present, not merely as survivals, but as equal factors in its power.'[20] Traditional moral and political codes retain much of their force, but they can no longer invest one's experience with sufficient meaning. The very survival of traditional moral norms allows one to measure how lamentably short of them most characters fall. Bart van Es sees *Hamlet* in such transitional terms, as a play 'divided between a feudal order (in which kingdoms are contested through single combat) and a modern world of *Realpolitik*, dominated by ambassadorial letters and secret deals. It has a ghost who suffers in medieval Catholic purgatory while his son returns from Wittenberg, the home of Luther and his new Protestant ideas.'[21] The philosopher Carl Schmitt writes of Shakespeare's hero as standing 'in the middle of the schism of Europe', at the crossroads between the old theology and the rise of the new nation-state.[22]

Imagine, then, a body of dramatic work which retains as compelling a sense of order as that of the ancient Greeks, along with the calamities which can result from breaching it, but which couples this passion for stability with a far keener, humanistic sense of the prodigal, inventive, potentially ruinous powers of the individual than one generally finds in ancient Athens. One then has some measure of the achievement of Shakespearian tragedy. Nowhere is this clash between order and disruption more obvious than in the poetry of the plays, which depends like any language on the regularities of grammar and logic, yet is so profuse and polyvalent that it threatens to undermine its own foundations. Shakespeare's belief in social order is jeopardised by the very language in which it is articulated. 'I can yield you [no reason] without words,' quips the Clown in *Twelfth Night*, 'and words are grown so false I am loath to prove reason with them'. Signs cut loose from their referents may then interbreed with other signs, rather as the Clown, having extracted one coin from Viola, asks slyly 'Would not a pair of these have bred, sir?' Money, like metaphor, is a magical power which can transmute anything into anything else, as Timon of Athens protests in a passage which attracted the attention of Karl Marx ('Thus much of this will make black white, foul fair, / Wrong right, base noble, old young, coward valiant . . .').

One problem with this circuit of exchange-value is that it threatens to level all rankings to a blank equality. It erases differences, spawns endless repetitions and reduces everything to a mirror-image of everything else. The interchangeability of the lovers of *A Midsummer's Night's Dream* is a case in point. What threatens to demolish social order is not only language and commerce but the anarchy of desire, for which all objects are purely contingent. In the end, *Eros* is secretly enraptured only by itself, like Orsino in *Twelfth Night*. Identity depends on mutuality, which is not what the new ethic of individual self-authoring maintains; yet there is a fine line between the reciprocity of selfhood which marks the traditional order and the arbitrary exchange of identities which belongs to the new. There is, remarks Ludwig Wittgenstein in his *Philosophical Investigations*, no more useless proposition than the identity of a thing with itself. Things in the plays which are wholly self-identical are ciphers which slip through the net of language and baffle all description. Yet exchange-value, in which the identity of an object lies outside itself in another object, and that in turn in another, is a form of 'bad infinity' to which the drama is constantly vigilant.[23]

Are meaning and value inherent in reality, or are they convenient fictions projected upon it? Shakespeare would seem to have his doubts about the naive subjectivism of a Troilus ('What's aught but as 'tis valued?'), along with the naturalistic doctrine (championed by a good many of his villains) for which the world is mere blank stuff to be bent to the ends of power, will and appetite. Men and women are self-fashioning animals able to forge their own history, and to do so may mean breaching customary restraints. It is of our nature to exceed ourselves. Overflowing the measure is built into what we are. So, too, is rejoicing in this superabundance for its own sake. Yet too lavish an excess, like too vaulting an ambition, may lead us to overreach ourselves and bring ourselves to nothing. Like Lady Macbeth, one can forget that constraints (the demands of kinship or hospitality, for example) are constitutive of the self, not simply obstacles to its expression. We must therefore be recalled like Lear to the finite nature of the flesh. Those who behave as entrepreneurs of the self, treating it simply as stuff to be exploited for their own private ends, are likely to come to grief; yet they are also harbingers of a future which is already at work undermining the pieties of the past.

'But I have that within which passeth show' (Act 1, sc. 2), protests Hamlet. We are witness here to the birth of a distinctively modern form of subjectivity – one which in its elusive, protean, impenetrably inward nature withstands all attempts to be cognitively grasped, as well as all demands to comply with social protocol. Revenge is a matter of tit-for-tat, and Hamlet's sense of himself as incommensurable refuses all such vulgar exchange-value. The symmetry of vengeance is at odds with the superfluity of his selfhood. If he is a poor actor, despite his fondness for the theatre, it is because he is incapable of sticking to a script – which is to say, to a pre-ordained version of himself, whether as lover, avenger or future monarch. The Hamlet-like self is sheer surplus and vacuity, so that for him to take determinate action would be to betray its unfathomable depths. Desire is infinite but the act a slave to limit, as Shakespeare's Troilus complains. So it is that Hamlet loiters on the edge of the symbolic order while never quite entering it, spurning sexual reproduction, brooding on the incest which disrupts all systems of kinship. It is no longer a question of whether individual freedom can be reconciled with the requirements of social order, but of whether there is not something inherent in subjectivity itself, grasped as a kind of *néant*, conundrum or 'bad infinity', which sets it against all social convention.

Shakespearian tragedy draws much of its strength from portraying with equal conviction the traditional order and the forces which threaten to usurp it. The former is no mere painted backdrop, while the forces of individualism can be productive as well as malign. For Jacobean tragedy in general, by contrast, the sense of a time-hallowed order is much less insistent, rather as Euripides is more sceptical of cosmic order than Aeschylus. That vision is available now only in stray tags or sporadic insights. Individual self-fulfilment declines into the squalid pursuit of self-promotion. We are presented with a dissolute, death-haunted world shorn of transcendence or inherent design, shot through with intrigue, paranoid sovereignty, false appearances, bottomless appetite and unbridled lust. The royal court is a centre of lawlessness rather than a hub of moral authority, and to be virtuous is to be victimised. In this realm of pampered, perverse desires, history is mere temporal decay, flesh, honour and allegiance are commodities to be bought and sold, and a deep desire for oblivion runs beneath the steady dissolution of meaning into savage farce. Human identities are as fractured as the broken-backed form of the plays themselves.

All this is staged with a sadistic delight in violence, grotesquerie and sensationalist spectacle – in extravagant violations of realism and shamelessly gratuitous devices which are to be consumed in 'decadent' style as ends in themselves. By contrast with Shakespeare, there is little constructive about the powers which the questioning of tradition has unleashed. Transition has become stalemate. If the future is not in the pocket of the new breed of possessive individualists, it is only because the very conception of historical progress has collapsed in the general erosion of meaning, to be replaced by the eternal repetitions of appetite, the clash of plot and counterplot and the sterile reciprocities of revenge.[24]

In Racinian tragedy, so Lucien Goldmann argues in *The Hidden God*, God is present and absent in the world simultaneously, and the same is true of the tragic protagonist. The Almighty has withdrawn from his Creation, turning his hinder parts to the purgatorial world he has created, and absolute value has consequently vanished. Yet its shadow still falls across a sterile reality, causing the protagonist to refuse the world in a quest for transcendence. Absolute value cannot be realised, but neither can its ghost be entirely exorcised. It is as though the Almighty lives on only in the form of a fruitless search for him or in the experience of guilt. The dilemma is that God's retreat from the world has drained it of merit; but it also means that this charnel house of a Creation is all there is, so one can neither embrace it nor spurn it for some higher sphere. Living in the world is unendurable, and it is the silence of the heavens which makes it so.

The tragic hero, then, is in Goldmann's view one who lives in the presence of an absent God, staggering under the burden of an absolute demand which makes no sense in worldly terms.[25] An increasingly rationalist social order can make nothing of such edicts, or provide the terms on which we might bow to their authority. Because God has become inscrutable, the question addressed to this elusive Other is the classical query of the hysteric: 'What am I to do? What is it you want of me?' The hysteric thus becomes exemplary of the human subject in general, confronted with an order which is no longer properly intelligible, let alone just. In this austere Protestant vision, spirit cannot become incarnate in the flesh. Value can exist in the human subject, but it cannot be realised in reality. In Simon Critchley's phrase, 'the truth of subjectivity has to be lived apart from the world'.[26] Torn between a lost world of immanent meaning and a rapacious regime of power and desire, the hero is destroyed.

One might trace this conflict in the very form of Racine's drama, not least in the extraordinary tension between the refinement of the verse and the turbulent stuff with which it deals. Some of these mannered patricians are also libidinal monsters. As George Steiner comments, 'A controlling poise is maintained between the cool severity of the technique and the passionate drive of the material.'[27] Formally speaking, the plays retain a deep-seated sense of order, but it is one which their content continually threatens to shatter. At a different level, however, form and content mirror each other in their stringent economy. One can find this compactness in the way the dramatic plots yoke opposing elements together – in their constant ironies, ambivalences, mismatchings, backfirings, self-undoings, cross-purposes, double dealings and self-divisions. All of this makes for a kind of negative symmetry, so that the neo-classical shapeliness of the plays is less a matter of harmony than of parallel frustrations. In *Andromache*, for example, Andromache loves her dead husband Hector, Pyrrhus loves Andromache, Hermione loves Pyrrhus and Orestes loves Hermione.

This unity of opposites is mirrored in the ironies and inversions of the verse. Hippolytus in *Phèdre* is 'dragged by the horses which his hands have fed' (Act 5, sc. 6); Orestes tells Andromache that 'I slay a king whom I revere' (Act 5, sc. 4); 'I have loved too well not to detest him now' (Act 2, sc. 1), Hermione remarks of Pyrrhus in *Andromache*; 'I embrace my rival, but it is to stifle him' (Act 4, sc. 3), comments Burrhus in *Britannicus*, while Britannicus himself speaks of Agrippine as having 'wed my father to bring about his ruin' (Act 1, sc. 4). The verbal texture of the plays is laden with such dialectical images, which serve as so many local examples of the way in which, on the larger scale of the plots themselves, it is compression – the airless enclosure of the world of the nobility – which helps to engender the conflict. In this sealed, thinly populated space, actions and their consequences form a mesh from whose toils no character can cut himself loose.

Economy at the level of form may appear as deftness and concision, but in the case of content it suggests a world in which everything has been ruthlessly stripped down to power and desire. It is logical that Racine's finest play, *Phèdre*, should turn on incestuous love, since incest, as we have seen, is among other things a matter of excessive economy, pressing the logic of this clique of aristocrats, many of them blood relations to each another, to an intolerable extreme. The language of the plays may be pared and polished, but it speaks of an *Eros* which is inherently anarchic. Moreover, love in this world of libidinal determinism is quite as pitiless and intemperate as hate, a condition into which it can capsize at any moment.

Love ravages and divides rather than heals and unifies, obeying its own merciless law and making those in whom it sinks its claws hateful and alien to themselves. In this realm of conflicting appetites, others must be either possessed or destroyed. In their quest for authenticity, no compromise is possible for the protagonists. A heroine such as Phèdre thus joins a tradition of tragic figures, from Oedipus, Philoctetes and Antigone to Samuel Richardson's Clarissa, Schiller's Karl Moor, Ibsen's Brand and Arthur Miller's Willy Loman, who are gripped by a demand quite as inexorable as the fate of classical antiquity. We have seen this already in the case of Antigone. Impelled by the force of *Thanatos*, they are driven first into solitude and then, typically, into death. What has replaced the Absolute is the relentless nature of the pursuit of it.

If this undertaking is bound to fail, it is not least because the demands placed on us by the psychopathic God of radical Protestantism, a God before whom we are always in the wrong, are as impossible to decipher as the bureaucratic workings of Franz Kafka's castle. Divine law is at once empty and imperious. It does not make sense, but one must submit to it even so. For it to be intelligible would bind it to the world of everyday reason, which would then spell the end of its transcendence. Given a value-free rationality, there is no basis in reason on which spiritual truths could be founded, so that as reason grows more lucid and precise, the sphere of spirit grows more cryptic and obscure. Value is banished beyond the borders of the empirical world; yet though this means that we can say little or nothing about it (hence the eloquent silence of the Racinian hero, as Goldmann sees it), its absence, like a distant cry of pain or horror, never ceases to haunt us.

Goldmann finds a historical context for Racine's tragic vision in a process of political transition, as the so-called *noblesse de robe* is displaced in seventeenth-century France by a centralised bureaucratic state, beating a disdainful retreat from what it sees as a degenerate world. A transition of a different kind underlies the great efflorescence of German drama in the late eighteenth century and the years after 1800. Goethe's *Götz von Berlichingen*, *Egmont*, *Iphigenia in Tauris* and *Torquato Tasso*, Schiller's *The Robbers*, *The Conspiracy of Fiesco in Genoa*, *Don Carlos*, *Wallenstein* and *Maria Stuart*, Kleist's *Penthesilea* and *Prince Friedrich von*

Homburg, Hölderlin's *The Death of Empedocles*: all these works belong to a history in tumult, on which Georg Büchner's *Danton's Death* offers a more belated reflection. Most of them are fables of autocracy and rebellion, freedom and fraternity, insurgency and absolutism, despotism and republicanism, whose chief protagonist in a Europe stumbling towards political revolution, or already caught up in its throes, is the idea of liberty. It is, as Schelling remarks, the alpha and omega of all philosophy. In Schiller's *Don Carlos*, the Marquis of Posa is a typically transitional figure – one who speaks up for republican freedom but who does so prematurely, and as a result meets his death at the hands of the state. Even so, the dynamic of history is stealthily at work on his side.

This body of drama is accompanied in the years around the turn of the eighteenth century by a new discourse known as the philosophy of tragedy. It marks a shift from tragedy to 'the tragic' – from the art-form itself to a more far-reaching political, religious and philosophical vision. If tragedy is the most 'philosophical' of artistic forms, meaning the one that in modern times has most regularly caught the eye of the philosophers, it is largely because it speaks of more than itself. It would hardly compel the attention of a Schelling or Hegel if it were simply a matter of flawed heroes or wrecked hopes. We shall see later that this theoretical current broods rather on the conflict between liberty and law, spirit and Nature, freedom and necessity, which it regards as the very essence of tragic art.

If these reflections are of an abstract kind, there is all the more need for them to be concretised by art. Philosophy can say, but art can show. Stephen Halliday argues that one reason for Plato's suspicion of tragedy is that he saw it as an embryonic form of philosophy, and thus as a major adversary to be faced down.[28] With the German Idealists, Plato's worst fears are belatedly realised. It is in the wake of the French Revolution, in the period from 1792 to 1807, that the theory of tragedy flourishes most abundantly, at a time when European history itself would seem to have taken a cataclysmic turn. Bloodshed on an epic scale is no longer confined to the stage of Seneca.

Transition is a vital concept in the theory of tragedy as much as in the theatre. In Hegel's view, Greek tragic art represents a specific stage in the unfolding of the World Spirit, as the limited religious and political outlook of classical antiquity gives way to a more modern world-view. A corporate notion of the ethical, one mediated by law and imposed by an external power, is supplanted by a more inward, individual morality. It is this momentous historical shift which the Hegel of *The Phenomenology of Spirit* finds above all in the clash between Creon and Antigone. As we shall see later, tragedy for Hegel plays a key role in resolving certain structural contradictions within ancient Greek civilisation: between the human and divine realms, for example, but also between the family, the female sphere and the private life on the one hand, which cherishes the notion of individuality, and the political state on the other, which threatens to negate it. 'The ethical life of the *polis*,' observes Rainer Friedrich, 'has no room for autonomous individuality.'[29]

If Spirit is to evolve, this clash between domestic and political spheres needs to be resolved; and tragedy has a strategic role to play this respect, allowing us an insight into the unity which underlies these apparently antithetical claims. The truth of opposition is identity. The true subject of tragic drama for Hegel is not this or that action or character but so-called ethical substance itself, which it shows to be ultimately indestructible. Like some ghastly stuff in science fiction, it is no sooner torn apart than it knits together again. In Hegel's view, the tragic art of ancient Greece also has what Joshua Billings calls 'a specific cognitive role in a specific historical moment: it is the medium through which ancient Greece becomes aware of the inadequacy of its form of religion', reconfiguring the relations between the human and the divine.[30] Tragedy is thus a way-station on the path to what Hegel sees as the only genuine resolution of this problem, namely Christianity, in some revisionist version of which he seems to have placed his faith.

Hölderlin, too, sees tragedy as an essentially transitional form. As in the work of his compatriot Walter Benjamin, it shows us the creation of a new order from the collapse of the old, a project to which the sacrificial death of the hero is pivotal. If that death signifies a defeat, it is also the catalyst of social transformation – a 'purifying death', as Holderlin has it, as a consequence of which the populace will rise up in revolt. Goethe's *Egmont* might serve as an illustration. In Hölderlin's view, we are speaking of an art concerned not with timeless truth but with constant disruption and renewal. In fact, Dionysus, the divine patron of tragedy, is regularly associated in Hölderlin's thought with historical upheaval. The pathos of the form lies in the fact that the new dispensation cannot be brought to birth without the annihilation of the old. Joshua Billings argues that the German poet finds in *Antigone* a passage from one form of politics and theology to another. A Creon-like view of the divine as mediated by law and political authority clashes with Antigone's own more intuitive rapport with the gods – a sense of divinity which looks defiantly to a more egalitarian, individualist age to come. It is a 'republican' future, as Hölderlin daringly calls it, one whose violent birth his own age was to witness. Ancient Greek tragedy becomes a foretaste of modern revolution.

Karl Marx was another who was acutely conscious of the relation between tragedy and transition. Like Hegel, he regards Goethe's *Götz von Berlichingen* as a tragically misplaced figure – a sixteenth-century scion of the aristocracy at war with a new, more cynical age of *Realpolitik*. As an advocate of such time-hallowed values as honesty and fidelity, Götz is brought low by an emergent social order for which power is in the process of outdating moral integrity. In Marx's view, something of the same applies to Ferdinand de Lasalle's tragic drama *Franz von Sickingen*, whose eponymous hero strikes against the status quo, but does so as the agent of a patrician class already in decline. As a spokesman for revolutionary ideas, he is in fact in the service of reactionary social interests.[31] There are also such premature revolutionaries as Thomas Müntzer, the subject of a classic study by Friedrich Engels, *The Peasant War in Germany*, who fail not because of their class background but because their political hour has not yet struck.

Walter Benjamin has a typically idiosyncratic view of the transitional nature of tragedy. The tragic hero, he argues in *The Origin of German Tragic Drama*, finds himself suspended between the old regime of myth and the gods and the birth of a new community, one which his sacrificial death will help to usher in. Belonging fully to neither order, and eventually crushed to death between them, he is caught between the language of ancient law and superstition and the as yet inexpressible discourse of the ethico-political future. As a sacrificial victim, the tragic hero is a remnant of the *ancien régime*; but he also represents a principle which is capable of bringing it low, and as such foreshadows an emancipated future. Poised at a point of violent passage between the one dispensation and the other, the hero refuses to justify himself in the eyes of the gods and accomplishes a breach with fate – with what Benjamin calls in his essay 'Fate and Character' 'the endless pagan chain of guilt and atonement', to which St Paul gives the name of the Law.[32] It is from this compulsive repetition, one in which it is not hard to detect the demonic presence of the death drive, that tragedy offers to set us free, as the hero transcends his fallen state through his sacrificial death and enters into communion with divinity. In an earlier essay, Benjamin sees the tragic protagonist as achieving a fulfilment which is possible only in Messianic rather than secular time, but since nobody can actually live in this mode of temporality, the hero must die – die, so to speak, of his own immortality, which removes him from the empty, eternally unfulfilled time we lesser mortals are forced to inhabit.[33]

Tragic art, then, stages a revolt against the Olympians, marking a shift from pagan ritual to the ethico-political, myth to truth, fate to freedom, Nature to history, the despotic sway of warring deities to a redeemed people. Yet in Benjamin's eyes the hero's insurgency is doomed to be premature. Unable to articulate a new form of communal existence, and powerless to escape the clutches of myth and destiny, he is condemned to an eloquent silence or moral speechlessness. If he is struck dumb, it is because he derives his identity from a social order yet to be born, which once it has sprung into being will learn its language from his muteness. As such, he has the elusive quality of all signifiers of utopia. Offering up his body to the ruling powers, he nevertheless preserves his soul intact and aloof, referring salvation forward to the future but, since he also shrinks from his death, this prospect offers him no great consolation.

Conscious of his moral superiority to the Olympians, the protagonist is unable to lend this awareness a tangible shape. All he can do in such unripe conditions is allow himself to be immolated by the community in order to placate the savagery of the gods. Through this ritual appeasement, those who slaughter him in the name of an oppressive past may come to acknowledge the injustice of the heavens, and in doing so turn their eyes to a liberated future. It is this project that Benjamin, inspired by Georg Lukács's *History and Class Consciousness*, will later translate into political terms, as the scapegoat of the proletariat, perpetually sacrificed to the ruling powers, no longer maintains its abject silence but becomes newly conscious of its victimised status. In doing so, it forges the terms of a new community and extricates itself from its bondage to myth, now renamed as ideology. (Ideology, Benjamin remarks, is a mode of thought that will survive as long as the last beggar.)

Martin Heidegger's *Introduction to Metaphysics* also sees tragedy as a transitional affair, but from a political standpoint antithetical to Benjamin's own. The tragic poet, for Heidegger, is an avant-garde transgressor who speaks of what has so far been unthought and unsaid, guided by the power of Being to devise a new world in the manner of a world-historical statesman (Heidegger presumably has Hitler in mind). He is an architect of myth rather than a critic of it. Great tragedy, then, is a revolutionary act of world-founding; and the unhappy fate of such world-founders, prophets out of joint with their times who are destined for martyrdom, is often enough the subject-matter of the drama itself.

For Timothy J. Reiss's ambitious, imaginative study *Tragedy and Truth*, tragic art stages an appearance when the social and political order is undergoing some profound reorganisation: the founding of the ancient Greek *polis* and the conflicts leading to the Peloponnesian wars, the formation of the modern nation-state and the religious battles of sixteenth-century Europe, the period of Romanticism and revolution and so on. Tragedy plays a key role in forming a system of concepts appropriate to such times of tumult, but it also shows up the limits of that knowledge, allowing us to sense certain meanings which it cannot incorporate. The tragic thus points to an excess or impossibility of meaning, one which eludes a given regime of knowledge, and in this sense is a radical force. Yet it also helps to regulate this potentially destabilising surplus. In reducing it to an established order of reference, rationality and representation, it earns the distrust of Foucauldians such as Reiss, for whom any such system smacks of oppression.

On the one hand, then, tragedy acts out the inexpressible at the heart of a social or discursive order. On the other hand, it helps to recuperate this unruly stuff for conventional knowledge, 'bring[ing] about rationality by showing what can be termed the irrational within that rationality'.[34] It is a way of neutralising the threat posed by the unintelligible. 'Tragedy,' Reiss observes, 'is both the moment of crisis and its resolution.'[35] A traditional view of tragedy as reconciliation is translated into the language of contemporary theory. Yet, whereas some earlier thinkers draw comfort from this settlement, Reiss, who treats all order and stability (indeed, all systematic knowledge) as darkly suspect, and whose study is laced with a dash of Michel Foucault's political pessimism, sees tragic art as a way of appropriating forces which might otherwise undermine it. It may be a persuasive account of the *Oresteia*, but hardly of *The White Devil* or *All for Love*.

Fredric Jameson sees artistic modernism as springing from a process of modernisation which has yet to run its course. Perry Anderson argues in similar vein that it is the impact of modernity on societies which remain in some respects pre-modern which accounts for much of modernist art's disruptive force.[36] Once the business of becoming modern is complete, modernism as an artistic movement tends to lapse from sight. By and large, it is the product of civilisations which in Max Weber's terms are increasingly 'disenchanted', but which are still richly furnished with myth, fable, folk tale and the supernatural. One can exploit these resources either as a refuge from the more distasteful features of modernity or as symbolic frameworks within which to make sense of it. The secular is not yet so well-entrenched as to have erased all traces of the sacred, among the most vital of which is art itself. For Martin Heidegger, only by mining such precious symbolic reserves can humanity be redeemed. We late moderns live in the throes of a transitional epoch, as the reign of metaphysics, Socratic rationalism and Western technology draws to a close and a new mythological culture struggles to be born. In this historic passage, the wisdom of the Greek tragedians will prove indispensable.

Modernism, then, is a transitional phenomenon, which is no doubt one reason why it is so well-stocked with instances of tragic art. It can be contrasted in this respect with its post-modern successor. In the drama of Ibsen and Chekhov, notions of freedom and enlightenment bred largely in the city have drifted to the countryside, to find themselves locked in combat with the stiff-necked mores of an entrenched rural order.[37] But that order, not least in the case of Chekhov, is dying on its feet, besieged by disruptive social and commercial forces, as the cherry orchard in the play of that title passes out of the possession of the landowning gentry into the pocket of a self-made businessman. We shall see later that being suspended in this way between past and future gives rise in some of Chekhov's characters to a degree of ironic self-awareness, as these cracker-barrel philosophers look wistfully to an emancipated future in which they know they will play no part, and which requires their own fading from the historical record. There may indeed be hope, but not for them. Trapped between a listless nostalgia for the past and a fruitless yearning for the future, these broken, burnt-out figures, their heads stuffed with trifles and half-remembered tags, live in a world of emotional stalemate. Tedium is as infectious as typhoid, and all sense of historical purpose has collapsed into sheer contingency. All one can now share with others is one's sense of solitude. Yet, in a triumph of dramatic form, the plays weave these plaintive voices and off-beat personalities into an exquisitely orchestrated whole. They are also held together by their remarkable consistency of mood.

There are characters in the theatre of Henrik Ibsen for whom the future is already dimly present – enlightened souls such as John Rosmer of *Rosmersholm*, whose progressive values are at odds with the pieties of conservative rural Norway. The problem, however, is that if the future is latent in the present, the past persists there too, so that the contemporary moment becomes the ground on which past and future meet in dead-lock, and men and women are crushed by their collision. If the obstacles to freedom were simply external – priggish parsons, crooked administrators, corrupt petty officials and the like – the situation would not be so dire. The truth, however, is that the drive for freedom is self-thwarting, eroded from the inside by the guilt and debt it accumulates. There can be no freedom without injury to others. The very sources of truth and liberty are polluted. August Strindberg shares much the same sombre vision in such pieces as *The Father* and *Easter*. And there are lethal legacies in the blood, not simply in society.

In the tightly meshed townships of the provinces, where individual lives are more closely interlinked than in the anonymous city, it would seem a law that self-fulfilment involves the sacrifice or betrayal of others. 'Men tear their way through a great many ties to get to their happiness,' remarks Miss Hessel in *Pillars of the Community*, which is one reason why that happiness continually turns to ashes in their mouths and the blitheness of the free spirit lapses into remorse and self-reproach. 'To be wholly oneself!' exclaims Ibsen's Brand. 'But how, with the weight of one's inheritance of sin?' Noble aspirations turn out to have their roots in crime and retribution – in moral debts and crippling obligations that can never be discharged. In this sense, Ibsen's theme from beginning to end is original sin. We are the heirs of a tainted legacy which we were never invited to choose, but which vitiates our actions at root. It is a condition prefigured in some Romantic tragedy, with its homeless, guilt-ridden, remorseful protagonists haunted by the nameless crime of being themselves. In Ibsen, the sources of one's identity are shady in both senses of the term: morally disreputable but also indeterminate, so that there are times when it is not clear whether a crime has been committed or not.[38] The same is true of the most Ibsenite of T.S. Eliot's plays, *The Family Reunion*. Bourgeois individualism assumes that one is the proprietor of one's destiny; yet in the tangled skein of human cause and effect, it is not always easy to say who owns an action, or whether one has acted at all, or whether what seems the result of your own initiative is a covertly collaborative affair. Perhaps one is both author and victim of events. Is it you or the past which determines your fate, and how far may trying to flee your fate send you hurtling towards it? If we are not far from the world of Oedipus, it is not only because he himself is caught in this contradiction, but because original sin is universal. The possibility of mutual harm is built into the interdependence of human beings.

The avant-garde impulse to break free of guilt by wiping the historical slate clean, clearing the space for a new start, is unmasked as a fantasy. There is always too much history for that. In terms of sheer bulk, the past has the edge over the present, and those who seek to shuck it off are themselves the products of it. Wiping the slate clean is itself an historical act. Victory, remarks Rosmer, is never won for a cause that has its roots in guilt; yet in the interwovenness of human lives, of which cause is this not true? Benjamin Constant speaks in his 'Reflections on Tragedy' of how the network of institutions 'which envelops us from our birth and is not broken until our death' is the modern equivalent of the fate of the ancients;[39] and nowhere is this more obvious than in Ibsen's theatre, where the dead hand of the past reaches out to crush the protagonist at the very moment he seeks to close his fist over truth, freedom, joy and innocence – ideals which are by no means to be spurned, but which are always compromised and contaminated.

Ibsen's work, writes Raymond Williams, reveals the tragedy of 'a man at the height of his powers and the limits of his strength, at once aspiring and being defeated, releasing and destroyed by his own energies'.[40] Much of its pathos springs from the fact that the defeat in question is not just an accident, as though the hero might have won through but happens to fail. On the contrary, it is the necessity of this failure which is so striking – the deadly dialectic by which freedom turns into bondage, self-fulfilment is bound up with self-hatred, truth is built on a lie and the dead determine the living quite as much as in the *Oresteia*. If the mountains are a symbol of freedom, their icy chill is also resonant of death. There is a social foundation to these contradictions. What is at stake here is the central dilemma of liberal society: the fact that my right to self-realisation is absolute, but by the same token so is yours, and it is not clear how a war to the death between us may consequently be averted. One holds oneself in sacred trust, so that Nora of *A Doll's House* must act on this merciless obligation to herself even if it means walking out on her children. To sacrifice the self, Irena protests in *When We Dead Awaken*, is an act of self-murder. Yet to insist on one's self-fulfilment may involve a mortal sin against others, as with a whole line of Ibsenite protagonists from Karsten Bernick to Arnold Rubek. As in the later fiction of Charles Dickens, it is crime which what lies at the root of achievement. The plays admire the audacious vision of the entrepreneur, the modern equivalent of the epic hero; but they are also well aware of the violence and lawlessness of these spiritual aristocrats, with their ruthless pursuit of self-interest and lordly contempt for the *canaille*.

'Two souls dwell in the breast of every complete bourgeois,' writes Werner Sombart, 'the soul of the entrepreneur and the soul of the respectable middle-class man . . . the spur of enterprise is a synthesis of the greed for gold, the desire for adventure, the love of exploration . . . [while] the bourgeois spirit is composed of calculation, careful policy, reasonableness and economy.'[41] Capitalist endeavour, in short, is at war with bourgeois morality. Yet it also needs this framework if it is to flourish. As Franco Moretti points out, Ibsen's drama turns not on the struggle between capital and labour but on a conflict *within* the middle class, between its pioneering, boldly transgressive captains of industry and its stiflingly respectable pastors and politicians.[42] Among other things, it is a contest between those who gaze eagerly to the future and those who remain imprisoned in the past. The priggish Rummel of *Pillars of the Community* voices the pious hope that 'the new enterprise [the railways] will not disturb the moral foundations on which we now stand', but these two aspects of middle-class society are not easy to reconcile. The entrepreneur is a reckless, freebooting adventurer with more than a touch of the outlaw about him, perpetually in danger of flouting the very norms which serve to legitimate his activity. Nietzsche, who has no regard for either social consensus or orthodox morality, is recklessly prepared to sacrifice these shibboleths to the infinite dynamism of the *Übermensch*, a figure who stoops to nobody's law but his own. For Hegel, all great lawgivers are also lawbreakers, harbingers of the future who are bound to seem delinquent in the eyes of the timorous present. Raskolnikov proposes much the same view in Dostoevsky's *Crime and Punishment*, at a time when the artist, criminal, adventurer and evil genius are becoming increasingly hard to tell apart.

Hilde Wangel of Ibsen's *The Master Builder* is a full-blooded Nietzschean, insisting that those of 'a strong conscience bursting with health' should hold fast to their desire without the slightest tincture of guilt or tremor of compunction. Ibsen admires this spiritual aristocratism, not least for its bravura and panache; yet, unlike Nietzsche, the harassed clerk, abused wife or down-at-heel engineer have as much claim on his imaginative sympathy as these more flamboyant trail-blazers of the human spirit, and part of the power of his theatre lies in its readiness to extend the status of tragedy to these unremarkable creatures. The same is true of the contemporaneous fiction of Thomas Hardy. Brand, Borkman, Hedda Gabler and Arnold Rubek of *When We Dead Awaken* are tragic protagonists in a classical sense of the term – hungry, demonically driven, larger-than-life seekers after power, truth or glory in social conditions too drearily petty-bourgeois to offer them much more than deadlock and disenchantment. Yet it is Ibsen's readiness to acknowledge the tragedy of less glamorous souls which marks him out from Calderón or Corneille. It is with his theatre above all that the phrase 'bourgeois tragedy' ceases to be a double oxymoron – double because the bourgeois vision is generally considered to be more bright-eyed than despondent, but also because tragedy is traditionally regarded as the preserve of gods, heroes and patricians rather than the province of medics, attorneys and accountants.

If the present is invaded by a past which blocks the possibility of a future, history would seem to logjam and the whole concept of linear development begins to unravel. There is something within the onward movement of the free spirit or visionary entrepreneur which threatens to undermine it, reducing narrative to stalemate, perpetual motion to eternal stasis. Since the obstacles to freedom are built into it – since, in the end, they are nothing less than yourself – it follows that victory and defeat, creation and destruction, fulfilment and frustration are synchronic rather than sequential. As Ulfheim remarks in *When We Dead Awaken*, 'you come to a tight corner where you can't go forward or back. And there you stick . . .' (Act 2). When the idea of transition is pressed to an extreme – when two contending orders, one dying and the other striving to be born, reach a point of deadlock – the result is likely to be an arrest or collapse of time itself, along with a loss of faith that its crimes and injustices can be redressed from within. So it is that naturalistic time in Ibsen's theatre comes to crisis in a dialectical image suspended between life and death, a moment in and out of time which signals both defeat and transcendence, as Rosmer and Rebekka step out to their *Liebestod* on the bridge over the millstream, Solness stands upright on top of his tower for a giddy moment of triumph before plunging to earth, the spiritually moribund Borkman climbs upward into the free air of the mountains to die in the snow, and Rubek and Irena scale the mountain peaks together to perish in an avalanche. The suicide of Rosmer and Rebekka signifies a renewed faith in the future, but it is also a capitulation to the benighted past. Much the same can be said of the endings of *John Gabriel Borkman* and *When We Dead Awaken*.

It will be left to a range of dramatists who write in Ibsen's wake to break with the naturalistic time-frame, opting instead for a stage on which this freezing of time can be directly dramatised. There will then be no more question of transition, since the very idea suggests a trust in linear evolution largely absent from the dream-like, disjointed narratives of Expressionist theatre, the sluggish temporality of a Chekhov, the dramatic montages of a Brecht or the plotless theatre pieces of a Beckett. Modernism itself may be a transitional phenomenon, but some of its works are in search of an eternal present, poised at the still point of the turning world where past, present and future are gathered into one. It is not as if history is hurtling towards catastrophe, but that it is no longer in motion at all.

We have seen that there are tragic dramas which are caught between an archaic, mythological world and a more rational, emancipated one. Jennifer Wallace sees some modern American tragedy in these terms, as immigrants from European cultures with ancient creeds and customs find themselves struggling to carve out a new identity for themselves in the perpetual present of the United States.[43] Albert Camus identifies two great tragic eras – that of ancient Greece, and a period which opens with Shakespeare and ends with Calderón and Racine. Both spans of history, he argues, are marked by 'a transition from forms of thought impregnated with the notions of divinity and holiness to forms inspired by individualistic and rationalistic concepts'.[44] In Lacanian terms, one might see this as a passage from the Imaginary to the Symbolic, as the sphere of images and intuitions gives way to the domain of law, reason and discourse, and the intimacies of the family yield to the impersonal sphere of the *polis*. One might even suggest that such works maintain something of an Oedipal relation to the past, struggling to free themselves from its authority but unable to shake its dust from their heels. The drive for liberation becomes entangled in what it seeks to escape. At a personal level, those who seek to enter the symbolic order must avoid being drawn back into the pre-political realm of blood ties and bonds of affection, evident most of all in the infant's intense attachment to its carer. It is this passage that Hamlet fails fully to accomplish. The question of transition, then, is not as remote as one might imagine from the subject of incest, which as we have seen is an abiding concern of tragic art.

4

FRUITFUL FALSEHOODS

Ideology as the rationalising of injustice or oppression is at least as old as the Book of Job, but it would seem to be with Plato that it first makes its appearance as the deliberate cultivation of false consciousness. Most ideology is not conspiratorial in this way. Many of the myths peddled to the common people are also believed by those who propagate them, though we shall be looking at one or two exceptions in a moment. Disseminating beliefs they know to be false is not how rulers typically remain in power, not least because they can always be caught out. One reason why politicians are evasive is because they are trying not to lie, for reasons of prudence rather than probity. There may, however, be no very clear distinction between conscious and unconscious fictions. In one of the finest of contemporary Irish dramas, Frank McGuinness's *Observe the Sons of Ulster Marching Towards the Somme*, Kenneth Piper, the play's gay, dissident, satirical outsider, ends up assuming leadership of his fellow soldiers, exhorting them into battle with an outburst of bellicose Ulster chauvinism. It is hard to decide whether Piper has finally been claimed by the dead hand of his family's imperial past or whether, as an accomplished performer, he is compassionately spinning a heroic fiction for young comrades who are about to be butchered. Does Piper believe in his own propaganda or does he not? Perhaps the opposition is not as clear-cut as it may appear.

In the third book of the *Republic*, Plato proposes a political myth so bold that even he seems discomfited by it. The idea is to persuade the rulers, soldiers and common people that their youth was a dream – that, while it appeared to them that they were being reared and educated in human society, they were in fact being formed in the womb of the earth and then disgorged into the upper world. Since the earth was both mother and nurse to them, they would feel duty bound to defend that region of it known as their homeland from assault. Curiously, then, the illusion in question consists of convincing the citizenry that they have been living an illusion. One wonders about the competence of an army and governing class credulous enough to swallow this noble lie, but there is still more implausible stuff to come. Citizens must also be informed that God has framed them in different ways, mingling gold with the composition of the rulers, silver with those destined to be auxiliaries, or aids to the ruling class, and brass and iron with the make-up of more menial types, and that nothing should be more jealously guarded than this mechanism of natural selection. If the son of a golden or silver parent is born with an admixture of brass or iron, he must be relegated without compunction to the lower ranks; but a meritocratic principle is at work too, since children of artisans born with some element of gold or silver may rise through the social hierarchy to assume their place as guardians or auxiliaries. Human beings are composed in part of natural materials which determine their social status, so that one would no more think of resenting one's own rank or that of others than one would feel aggrieved by the twinkling of a star. It is ideology as 'naturalising' in the most literal of senses.

In Plato's ideal social order, the rulers would be granted a monopoly on lying. They would be allowed to utter falsehoods for the sake of the public good, but would penalise anyone else who was caught doing so. For a number of post-Platonic thinkers, what rulers need to keep secret above all is not the provenance of individual citizens but the unsavoury origins of political power. Most states are the upshot of war, invasion, revolution or extermination, a primordial trespass which it is vital to conceal from those who may need to be enlisted in defence of the realm. The original sin of sovereignty threatens to contaminate the history which flows from it, and so must be suppressed. What if law and order were no more than the result of collective amnesia, as the unlovely sources of authority are thrust deep into the political unconscious?

If we investigate the origins of nations, warns David Hume, we are bound to find rebellion and usurpation. 'Time alone,' he writes, 'gives solidity to [the rulers'] right; and operating gradually on the minds of men, reconciles them to any authority, and makes it seem just and reasonable.'[1] For Edmund Burke, hegemony is also a question of the passage of the years. 'Time,' he writes, 'has, by degrees . . . blended and coalited the conquered with the conquerors . . .'[2] If he is outraged by the French Revolution, it is not least because 'all the pleasing illusions which made power gentle, and obedience liberal . . . are to be dissolved by the new conquering empire of light and reason. All the decent drapery of life is to be rudely torn off.'[3] Power in Burke's view must beguile the senses, breeding noble deceptions and edifying fictions. It is uplift and consolation the populace needs, not truth. 'A wise man,' observes Matthew Arnold of the origins of property and the state, 'will not approve the violences of a time of confiscation; but, if things settle down, he would never think of proposing counter-confiscation as an atonement for those violences. It is far better that things should settle down, and that the past should be forgotten.'[4] Once the primal crime of nationhood is buried in the past, we can all come to be pleasantly oblivious of it. The violence which established the state in the first place is now sublimated into the military defence of it. Political hegemony is the fruit of fading memory. A nation, observes Ernest Renan, is defined as much as by what it forgets as by what it remembers. In Friedrich Schiller's drama *Wallenstein*, the protagonist comments that 'The march of years has power to sanctify; / Whatever's grey with age, men will call holy. / Once in possession, you are in the right' (Act 1, sc. 4).

Montaigne scoffs at abstruse inquiries into such matters, while Pascal warns in his *Pensées* that 'the truth about the [original] usurpation must not be made apparent: it came about originally without reason and has become reasonable. We must see that it is regarded as authentic and eternal, and its origins must be hidden if we do not want it soon to end.'[5] In this respect at least, one does not need to speak truth to power because power knows the truth already. Immanuel Kant also considers speculation on the sources of political authority to be a menace to the state.[6] 'Cheerfulness, the good conscience, the joyful deed, confidence in the future,' declares Friedrich Nietzsche, '– all of them depend on the existence of a dark line dividing the bright and discernible from the unilluminable and dark; on one's being just as able to forget at the right time as to remember at the right time . . .'[7] In his *Considérations sur la France*, Joseph-Marie de Maistre argues that political power survives only as long as its sources are cloaked in mystery. For this purpose, he advocates the diffusion of useful fictions among the populace, who are in any case incapable of living by anything but error. They must be persuaded to submit to the absolute authority of altar and throne, no matter how brutal or benighted these powers may be.

The other scandal to be kept from the ears of the masses is the fact that God, the foundation of moral value and social order, does not exist – or, if he does, that his powers have been drastically overestimated.[8] The piety of the people must be insulated from the scepticism of the intelligentsia. Voltaire, who thought that the multitude would always be benighted, was anxious that his domestic servants should not be infected by his own religious heterodoxy. In his theological tract *Pantheisticon*, the Irish philosopher John Toland (a radical, no less) insists that the truths of Reason must be kept remote from the superstitions of the mob. David Hume is equally aware of the gulf between the learned and the ignorant on these questions, but holds that a moderate version of religion, one which he does not believe in himself, may be an aid to political stability.[9] Thomas Jefferson also maintains that faith in God is vital for social cohesion, even though it was not a faith he shared. The equally godless Edward Gibbon holds much the same view.

Max Weber remarks in his celebrated essay 'Science as a Vocation' that only a plucky few can accept that the world has no inherent meaning, and that for those timorous souls who shrink from this truth 'the doors of the old churches are open widely and compassionately'.[10] The same concern to conceal the fact that moral values have no firm foundation can be found in the writings of the Nazi political theorist Carl Schmitt and the neo-conservative thinker Leo Strauss. Citizen and philosopher must be kept strictly apart. Given that human-kind cannot bear very much reality, civilisation for all of these thinkers depends on the sedulous cultivation of false consciousness. Only a carefully sustained conspiracy can buy off radical rationalism and political disaffection. The metaphysical bent of the masses is their rulers' insurance policy. It is a policy likely to deliver substantial benefits, since according to La Rochefoucauld, an author who prides himself on being hard to hoodwink, 'some disguised falsehoods are so like truths, that it would be judging ill not to be deceived by them'.[11]

It would be left to Nietzsche to call the bluff of the governing powers on the question of the Deity but, since he has no more faith than Voltaire or Friedrich Schiller that the common people could be enlightened on this score, or indeed on any other, his theatrical announcement of the death of God is as politically sterile as it is philosophically striking. In fact, he, too, despite denouncing Plato's noble lie in *The Will to Power*, speaks up for the pieties of the people – not, to be sure, in the interests of social order, and not simply because the plebs may be allowed to stew in the juice of their own ignorance, but because it is from austerity and self-sacrifice that the *Übermensch* will learn his self-discipline, and the Christian faith has at least delivered this. One must submit to such a moral regime in order to rise above morality altogether. So it is that one of Christianity's most eloquent adversaries is apparently content to see his fellow citizens climbing devoutly into their pews.

Plato may seek to bamboozle the masses with his fairy tales, but he also believes that they are mystified in any case, sunk in unreflective prejudice (*doxa*) rather than living by the steady light of truth. For Spinoza, who takes an equally demeaning view of the common folk, those who do not live according to reason occupy an imaginary sphere in which they judge the world only according to their own needs, appetites, affections and aversions. They are to be governed through myth and symbol, and ought not to try reading works such as Spinoza's own since they are bound to misinterpret them. Only reason will allow us to leap out of our own skins and see things as they are. Only by contemplating the world *sub specie aeternitatis* can we be released from the ravages of time and the despotism of desire. Anthropocentrism is the natural state of humanity, rather as the urge to self-preservation is its biological condition. This self-centredness follows from our existence as material bodies, judging things not by the eternal law of reason but according to how they delight or disgust our senses. In this sense, the paradigm of everyday experience is art, which makes no bones about grasping the world from a sensory, subjective angle.

One of the most deep-seated fantasies for Spinoza is the belief that we could act other than we do, given that he himself is a full-blooded determinist for whom freedom is the *apatheia* or serenity of mind which springs from knowing that things could not be different. To be truly free is to grasp the necessity of what we see around us, and in doing so to augment our power over the world. It is because the masses are ignorant of real causes that they mistake their own volition for the source of their actions. When it comes to the common order of nature, the mind has only a 'confused and mutilated'[12] knowledge of itself, the body and other material objects. Where Spinoza differs from Plato, however, is in his faith that this ignorance can be remedied. The populace need not be mired in delusion. Their desires are malleable enough to be remoulded, and it is this task, rather than the fostering of politically opportune fictions, that falls to the enlightened philosopher.

It was on account of this faith that Spinoza's name was feared and reviled among the governing classes of Europe. Condorcet found himself in agreement with his Dutch colleague: 'What morality can really be expected,' he inquires, 'from a system one of whose principles was that the morality of the people must be founded on false opinions, that enlightened men were right to deceive others provided that they supply them with useful errors, and that they may justifiably keep them in the chains that they themselves knew how to break?'[13] It is a succinct summary of the whole discreditable enterprise. Condorcet's heir in this respect is Sigmund Freud, who in *The Future of an Illusion* dismisses religious notions as fairy tales told to infants, and who in his late-Enlightenment style contemplates a future which would dispense with such opiate. The fact that a degree of delusion is constitutive of the ego need not entail a belief in goblins or weeping statues of the Virgin.

Perhaps neuroscience is the contemporary equivalent of Spinozist determinism. Rarely has the notion of freedom been so popular in practice and so suspect in theory. The general citizenry assume they are free, while a small band of geneticists and neuroscientists view their behaviour as the effect of neural firings or genetic inheritance, and their consciousness as an illusion. Yet rather as there were closet atheists in Victorian England who slipped into church for the sake of social stability, so these men and women behave in ways which might be considered to contradict their own scientific doctrines. Human society on this view is a contrivance in which we suspend our scepticism of free will and pitch in with the befuddled, freedom-loving masses for the sake of a quiet life. As with David Hume, too much theoretical speculation is likely to bring social existence grinding to a halt.

What is falsifying for Spinoza is not so much a corpus of myths as lived experience itself, which will grant us no access to eternal truth. The same is true for the left-Spinozist Louis Althusser, for whom ideology offers no access to the realm of Science or Theory. As with Kant's phenomenal and noumenal spheres, we live in divided and distinguished worlds, one of which – the territory of the 'lived' – is an indispensable fiction. Experience is no sure guide to the truth, whatever the empiricists may imagine. The sun may appear to be only a few miles away, but the astronomers inform us that things are otherwise. Not only that but, as Spinoza points out in the *Ethics*, our knowledge of the sun's actual distance from the Earth does nothing to dispel this perception. Truth and experience are separate domains. Truth does not automatically banish error, as a more militant form of rationalism would claim. Our minds may be open to reason, but our senses are not. The nature of truth runs counter to our corporeality. There is indeed absolute truth for both Plato and Spinoza, but it is not to be found in the phenomenological sphere.

The world for Spinoza appears to centre benignly on the human subject, even though reason informs us that it is icily indifferent to it. What we fondly imagine to be a loving parent is in fact a scandalously negligent one. There is something infantile about this condition, but it is not an infantilism we could ever hope to outgrow. As long as there is experience there will be misperception, which is why for Althusser (for whom experience is the name we give to our ideologies), ideology is eternal.[14] It is the very form of our experience, not simply (as with Plato's noble lie) its contents, which is the source of our misconceptions. In the imaginary bond between subject and world, the subject in Althusser's view comes to feel that reality has a claim on it – that it has foreseen its coming, prepared a special place for it and granted it a purpose and identity. Like a smooth-talking lover, the world in the shape of a dominant social order beguiles us into believing that it has need of us. Our existence no longer seems contingent, rather as the soldiers and statesmen of Plato's myth did not simply stumble by chance upon their vocations but were nurtured for them in the womb of Mother Earth. And since the ruling order has need of our active support, it sets us up as free agents. We come to see ourselves as the source of our own actions, even though Theory understands that we are simply the effect of this or that set of structures.

Althusser's theory of ideology mixes a dash of Spinoza with a touch of Schopenhauer, Nietzsche and Freud. For this line of thought, human action itself is a fruitful fiction. It depends on a groundless faith in the unity of the self. This unity may be the product of the Will (Schopenhauer), the practical needs of the species (Nietzsche), the ego (Freud) or ideology (Althusser). In all these cases we enjoy a sense of freedom and autonomy, so that the cunning of the forces which determine us lies in their ability to efface themselves. It is in this way that the human subject becomes coherent enough to act purposively. There are, to be sure, those superior minds which see through this subterfuge. 'When we have fully discovered the scientific laws that govern life,' comments Oscar Wilde, 'we shall realise that the one person who has more illusions than the dreamer is the man of action.'[15] When man acts, he remarks in *The Critic as Artist*, he is a puppet; when he describes he is a poet. Yet those who fail to act, such as Martin Decoud in Joseph Conrad's *Nostromo*, will catch themselves harbouring doubts about their own existence and gradually disintegrate. The choice between puppet and poet is one between self-deception and deception as an art-form. Lying for Wilde is one of the finest embellishments of everyday life. The aim of the liar 'is simply to charm, to delight, to give pleasure. He is the very basis of civilised society.'[16] Truth is for shopkeepers and the positivistic English.

The subject for Spinoza is unreasonable, though not (as for Nietzsche) unreal. To know the truth means eliminating it from the scene of knowledge, rather as Theory or Science for Althusser is a process without a subject. In the sphere of reason, subjectivity shows up simply as a blank. As Roger Scruton remarks, 'Spinoza can find no way to insert, into the heart of his universe, the subjective viewpoint from which it is surveyed.'[17] For Kant, by contrast, the world is inescapably *my* world. In Spinoza's view, misperception does not spring from things being reified, naturalised, sublimated, obfuscated or rationalised away, but simply from the fact that they are spontaneously present to a subject. The problem is not a defective subjectivity, but subjectivity as such.

Schopenhauer, for whom the malign Will warps all of our representations out of true, argues a similar case in more grandly metaphysical style, while Nietzsche continues to proclaim it in his wake. Who says consciousness says false consciousness. If to be aware is a blessing, it is not least because of the abundant opportunities for self-deception it provides, as well as the myriad ways in which we can mystify others. As the blind beggar Mary Doul complains in J.M. Synge's play *The Well of the Saints*, 'they're a bad lot those that have their sight, and they do have great joy, the time they do be seeing a grand thing, to let on they don't see it at all, and to be telling fool's lies . . .'[18] You can use your powers of discernment to dupe others, a deceit made easier by the fact that fantasy is what we live by. It is not an alternative to reality, but the very frame within which we conceive it.

In Hegel's view, error is constitutive of Spirit, whose blunders and oversights are vital to its unfolding. As Ulrich muses in Robert Musil's novel *The Man Without Qualities*, 'there was inherent in the course of history a certain element of going off course'. For *The Phenomenology of Spirit*, falsehood involves a distinction between knowledge and its object, but this is an essential condition of truth as well. Error is part of truth, since it counts among the materials on which it goes to work.[19] John Roberts writes of Hegel's belief in 'the endless capacity of humans to work through misrecognitions, errors and misconstruals, as a condition of the recovery and renewal of truth'.[20] One arrives at enlightenment only by the most circuitous of routes. In order to come into its own, the Idea must undergo *kenosis* or self-emptying, rather like the Father in the person of Christ.

Marx, too, is aware of the necessity of error, at least in certain social conditions. In his earlier work, false consciousness is necessary to mask and legitimate ruling-class power.

Fruitful falsehoods have the name of ideology. In his later writings, by contrast, distortion lies more on the side of the object than of the subject. Under capitalist conditions, semblance is built into substance, untruth is constitutive of truth and false appearances are an integral part of reality. There is a duplicity about the workings of the capitalist mode of production, which has nothing to do with subjective misconceptions. The wage-contract, for example, presents itself as an equal exchange, thereby concealing the reality of exploitation; the abstract equality of citizens in the political sphere belies their actual inequalities in civil society; and the commodities which appear to be the servants of humanity are secretly their masters. Rather like Nietzsche's Will to Power, the Real of the capitalist world spontaneously presents itself other than it is, and only the hermeneutic of suspicion known as science can lay bare the mechanisms by which reality systematically misinterprets itself. In Marx's view, there would be no need for such science if phenomena coincided with their essences.

In the work of Freud, the truth of the subject does not coincide with the knowledge of the ego. 'I am not where I think, and I think where I am not' is Jacques Lacan's memorable rewriting of the Cartesian cogito. 'The self, the place where we live, is a place of illusion,' writes Iris Murdoch.[21] What dispels this illusion in her view is art and the practice of virtue, both of which demand a selfless attention to the real. For Freud, by contrast, a new science (psychoanalysis) is needed if the gap between ego and unconscious is to be overcome. The ego itself is a form of life-lie, which thrives on a repression of the Real. Slavoj Žižek argues that there is a primordial fantasy which acts as the transcendental frame of consciousness – which is older than truth itself, and which constitutes the sustaining core of the subject.[22] Besides, it is through dream and fantasy that the truth of the subject speaks most eloquently, as well as being inscribed on the body itself in the neurotic symptom.

It is not only science that can bridge the gap between appearance and reality. The same is true of virtue. Since virtuous men and women are distinguished by a lack of hypocrisy, we are able – in the words of *Macbeth* – to find the mind's construction in the face. It belongs to moral integrity to manifest itself. This, however, is not the case for Niccolò Machiavelli, whose ideal ruler in *The Prince* must act ruthlessly from time to time but would quickly lose credibility were this to be apparent to the populace. It is not necessary for the prince to be righteous, but it is imperative for him to appear so. A hiatus between virtue and power thus gives rise to a gap between appearance and reality. Truth can no longer be entirely transparent. Traditional notions of virtue are still potent enough to command assent, though not authoritative enough to guide one's behaviour. 'Is' and 'ought' are misaligned, as political necessity threatens to discredit the very ethical codes to which it appeals. The clash in question is not one between private and public values, but between the formal and informal public spheres.

Fiction and dissimulation are now constitutive of political life, not occasional blemishes on it. All power contains an admixture of illusion. Machiavelli, to be sure, is no deep-dyed Machiavellian: rulers should behave well when it is possible for them to do so. Yet, as Quentin Skinner remarks, 'the problem is how to avoid appearing wicked when you cannot avoid behaving wickedly'.[23] It is fortunate in this respect that most men and women are easily duped, indeed are eager to allow themselves to be so. At the same time, religion can be exploited as ideology, inspiring citizens to put the good of the community above all other ends.

One of the most dedicated spinners of philosophical fictions is David Hume, who threatens to reduce knowledge to mere hypothesis, belief to a peculiar intensity of feeling, morality to sheer sentiment, causality to an imaginative construct and history to an indefinitely interpretable text. An idea which is held to be true simply feels different from a false one. Reasoning, Hume claims in his *Treatise of Human Nature*, is nothing but a form of sentiment consequent upon custom, and belief no more than a peculiarly vivid conception. Continuous identity is a phenomenon we can feel but not demonstrate, and causality is the effect of an imaginative expectation bred by habit. In fact, the imagination ('an inconsistent and fallacious principle' in Hume's view) lies at the source of all our knowledge, as well as being the ultimate arbiter of all philosophical systems. This capricious faculty also lies at the foundation of private property and the political state, as it does of memory and understanding. Not until the advent of Romanticism will this modest capacity be made to do so much hard labour.

Theory and practice are mutually at odds, since it is only by suppressing these subversive reflections that social existence can seem well-founded. The metaphysically minded masses assume that there are indisputable truths, whereas the sceptical theorists are glumly aware that there is nothing more solid than custom, sentiment, intuition and imagination. As the metaphysical ground crumbles beneath his feet, Hume manages in a moment of *mauvaise foi* to retreat into the carefully cultivated false consciousness of the coffee house, where by playing a little backgammon and making merry with his friends he can consign his doubts to politically convenient oblivion. There is no terra firma beneath our feet, but we must act as though there is.

Plato, Machiavelli, Voltaire and most other purveyors of convenient fictions do not intend to legitimate lying as such. Deceptions are regrettable, and should be diffused among the masses only when this is politically indispensable. They function within a general regime of truth, the foundations of which they do nothing to sabotage. Indeed, a lie pays homage to truth by masquerading as it. The thinker for whom lies are by no means lamentable necessities is Nietzsche, who is intent on reversing the values commonly assigned to truth and falsehood, and who is boldfaced enough to sing the praises of the fraudulent. 'It does seem,' he remarks in *The Joyful Wisdom*, 'as if life were laid out with a view to appearances, I mean, with a view to error, deceit, dissimulation, delusion, self-delusion . . .'[24] In *The Genealogy of Morals* he despises those who don't tell lies, scoffing that 'a real lie, a genuine, resolute, "honest" lie (on whose value one should consult Plato) would be something far too severe and potent for them'.[25] Truth is absurdly overrated, and can prove far less efficacious than falsehood. In our zealous pursuit of this ideal, we forget to inquire after its value. As John Gray comments in Nietzschean vein, there is a case that 'truth has no systematic advantage over error' in the course of human evolution.[26] Human beings on this view cannot live without illusion. Abjuring false judgements, Nietzsche claims in *Beyond Good and Evil*, would mean renouncing life itself. Falsehood is a condition of existence, and those who insist on looking the truth in the eyes are likely to end up perishing of it. Only an arbitrary prejudice persuades us that this perilous stuff is worth more than sheer semblance. The intellect, as with Schopenhauer, is a dissimulating organ in its very essence. The will to truth can prove devastating, the truth itself is ugly, and to demand it at any price is a form of madness. Truth has the power to annihilate, whereas fantasy is able to cherish and preserve. Our hunger for truth conflicts with our more fundamental need for fabrication, one which lies at the foundation of everything good and beautiful. What was previously a special case (the saving illusion) has now become a general epistemology.

To speak of falsehood is naturally to invoke some notion of truth. There are times, however, when Nietzsche appears to insist that truth itself is nothing but a productive misconception. Human truths, he comments in *The Genealogy of Morals*, are merely 'irrefutable errors' – the kind of contrivances, as he puts it in *The Will to Power*, without which a certain animal species could not survive. They are chimeras which we have ceased to recognise as such, metaphors which we have come to take literally. Truths are simply illusions which have outgrown their awareness of the fact. In the terms of Frank Kermode's *The Sense of an Ending*, they are myths rather than fictions, which are conscious of their own artifice. Yet if untruths can be life-enhancing, facilitating our dealings with the world and allowing us to master enough of it to survive and flourish, then Nietzsche cannot strictly speaking be a pragmatist. For most pragmatists, it is exactly such ideas which count as true, whereas to call them false suggests that one can assess their validity by some other criterion. For pragmatism, ideas are not false but fruitful, but fruitful (in some suitably sophisticated sense of the term) and therefore true.[27] On this view, there can be no fruitful falsehoods.

So does Nietzsche hold that there is no truth at all, or that truth exists but that it is inferior to illusion, or that it is simply useful error? Yet error in comparison to what? The Spirit of

Gravity in *Thus Spake Zarathustra* claims that all truth is twisted, but how could we possibly know this? How could the whole of our experience be out of kilter? It is doubtful, however, that Nietzsche rejects the idea of truth *tout court*. Along with the rest of humankind, he seems to acknowledge that veridical propositions are possible from time to time. Their truth-value, however, is relative to historically specific forms of discourse – regimes of truth, as Michel Foucault would say, which carve up reality in a variety of ways according to our material needs. Truth is anthropocentric. There is no iron-clad form of it, but there are approximate verities all the same. Even then, one can describe such truths as errors in so far as they can never be absolute. They are ultimately doomed attempts to nail down an unfathomably intricate reality, which is anyway in perpetual flux.

Besides, they can do this only by schematising, falsifying, stereotyping and oversimplifying in order to come up with a world which is calculable and manageable. Truth is fabricated rather than revealed, and everyday experience is thus more like an artefact than we imagine. Human beings in Nietzsche's view are natural-born liars – which is to say, rather more charitably, that they are natural-born artists. Truths are hermeneutical events, and there is in principle no end to the business of interpretation. It remains to be seen whether the human organism, having incorporated untruth into its existence in order to survive and flourish, will now be able to incorporate the truth – namely, the recognition that there is no truth, at least in any well-founded sense of the term. Only the *Übermensch* will prove equal to this challenge.

In a world of appearances, one thing stands out for its wondrous lack of reality: art. In an astonishingly bold gesture, Nietzsche severs the time-honoured link between art and truth. It is true that as an outburst of Dionysian energy, art can give us access to the Real. Yet, because the Real is terrible to behold, the function of art is to cloak it in the guise of the Apollonian. Rarely has a renowned philosopher of art been so brutally candid about the nature of art as opiate or of culture as false consolation. It is in dream and fantasy (the Apollonian) that the truth of the unconscious (the Dionysian) reveals itself, as it is for Freud, but only in displaced, discreetly tempered form. And since we would have no art without the savagery it sublimates, the finest flowers of civilisation have their roots in barbarism. It is a species of theodicy: cruelty and exploitation are unavoidable if history is to bring forth its Goethes and Tolstoys.

The Romantics and Idealists are mistaken to see art as a cognitive power. On the contrary, it is almost the opposite. 'Conscious of the truth he has once seen,' Nietzsche writes in *The Birth of Tragedy*, 'man now sees everywhere only the horror or absurdity of existence . . . he is nauseated. Here, where the danger to his will is greatest, *art* approaches as a saving sorceress, expert in healing. She alone knows how to turn these nauseous thoughts about the horror or absurdity of existence into notions with which one can live . . .'[28] It is a case which will become a cliché of modernism: reality is inherently chaotic, and only an arbitrarily imposed form can invest it with order. The world may be an illusion of a kind, but art (not least tragedy) is a *redemptive* illusion – a therapeutic fiction which allows us to live freely and exuberantly. Under cover of its formal composure, we can reap obscene enjoyment from the brute meaninglessness which lies at the root of reality. It is thus that Nietzsche claims in *The Birth of Tragedy* that only as an aesthetic phenomenon can existence be justified.

Art, then, represents a 'cult of the untrue' (*The Gay Science*) which schools us in an acceptance of semblance. We are reconciled to the fact that deception is a crucial condition of human life. We are also cured of the desire to explore metaphysical depths, which are simply the specious projection of surfaces. 'Truth is ugly', Nietzsche comments in *The Will to Power*. 'We possess art lest we perish of the truth.'[29] Genuine knowledge paralyses action, as we peer into the heart of things and are traumatised by the horrors we find lurking there. If we are to act constructively, it can only be by a certain salutary self-blindness. Theory and practice, for Nietzsche as for Hume, are mutually at odds.

The counterfeit nature of art is true to the falsity of the world; yet it is also false to this falsity, stamping some fleeting stability on its perpetual disorder. In giving expression to the

Will to Power, which is quite without sense or purpose, it also conceals this non-sense by the creation of form, which as we shall see in a moment is what the *Übermensch* does as well. Art is *determinate* illusion – illusion to the second power, so to speak, and as such is both symptom of and shield against the terrible (un)truth of the universe. It involves a double deception, since it conceals this (un)truth as well as giving voice to it. In its shapeliness of form, it is untrue to the only thing in the cosmos which is real, namely the Will to Power, which knows no such unity; yet this mercurial force is itself no more than a constant dissembling, determining itself differently at every place and time in a constantly fluctuating ratio of forces. 'The activity of life,' writes Gilles Deleuze, 'is like a power of falsehood, of duping, dissimulating, dazzling and seducing. But, in order to be brought into effect, this power of falsehood must be selected, redoubled or repeated and thus elevated to a higher power.'[30] It is art which performs this task.

Art is in this sense illusion: the consecration of a lie. Yet it is not simply illusion, since it is also a transformative, life-enhancing power, the kind of fertile misconception by which we can grow and prosper. This is particularly true of tragedy. 'Tragedy,' writes Gorgias the Sophist, 'by means of legends and emotions, creates a deception in which the deceiver is more honest than the non-deceiver and the deceived is wiser than the non-deceived.'[31] For Nietzsche, the tragic is the process by which terror can be alchemised into triumph without being denied. Even so, art is a means to human flourishing rather than an end in itself. Here again, Nietzsche is rare among aestheticians, this time in his frankly instrumental attitude to the art-work. He compensates for this streak of philistinism, however, by regarding the universe itself as a supreme fiction – an eternally self-generating, self-founding artefact which plays out its pointless game of pleasure with itself with no *telos* in sight. The world is a work of art which gives birth to itself, and it is by tapping into this process of free self-production, becoming a microcosm of the cosmos, that the *Übermensch* can achieve dominion over himself.

The *Übermensch* is a heroic self-fashioner – a self-mastering creature who hammers himself into stylish, aesthetically gratifying shape, living in experimental mode and acting only in accordance with the law of his own being. This post-human animal reinvents himself from moment to moment out of a superabundance of power and high spirits, stamping a shape on the turmoil of reality and the unruliness of his own desires. It is in this way that he compels his own chaos to become form. He is the work of art come magnificently alive, as artist, artefact and raw material in a single body; and like any other aesthetic creation his existence is entirely baseless. Like Kierkegaard's knight of faith, he is one of those rare human beings who have the courage to embark on the most perilous business of all – that of individuation. As a character in Ibsen's *Brand* remarks, the surest way to destroy a man is to turn him into an individual.

Hans Vaihinger's once influential study *The Philosophy of 'As If'* takes its cue from Nietzsche in treating ideas as instruments in the service of the will to live.[32] In Vaihinger's view, such ideas are fictional in nature and biological in origin. They provide us not with objective truth, but with the equipment we need for negotiating the world more effectively. They thus have a bearing on what Georges Sorel's *Reflections on Violence* (1908) calls a myth, meaning a body of images whose literal truth or falsehood is beside the point, but which expresses in symbolic form the collective experience of a group, and does so in order to inspire them to fruitful action. For Sorel, however, it is not as though the truth is patiently standing by, awaiting its symbolic expression; it is rather that the symbolic expression brings it to birth, just as for Oscar Wilde and W.B. Yeats it is only by adopting a mask that we can be ourselves. Primary among such fictions for Sorel are the ideas of political insurrection and the General Strike, imaginative fables 'which, b*y intuition alone*, and before any considered analyses are made, [are] capable of evoking as an individual whole the mass of sentiments which corresponds to the different manifestations of the war undertaken by Socialism against modern society'.[33] 'These myths,' Sorel maintains, 'are not descriptions of things but expressions of a determination to act,' and as such are closed to all refutation.[34]

The critic I.A. Richards argues in similar vein in *Mencius on the Mind* (1932) that we may be forced 'to supplement scientific psychology with a fictional account of human nature in the interests of a finely ordered society and of reasonably unwasteful living'.[35] 'Without his mythologies,' he writes elsewhere, 'man is only a cruel animal without a soul.'[36] Richards' pupil William Empson remarks that the problem of the modern age is that 'true beliefs may make it impossible to act rightly; that we cannot think without verbal fictions; that they must not be taken for true beliefs, and yet must be taken seriously'.[37] 'The final belief,' writes Wallace Stevens, 'is to believe in a fiction, which you know to be a fiction, there being nothing else. The exquisite truth is to know that it is a fiction and that you believe in it willingly.'[38] The later Heidegger presses this case a step or two further: untruth is more primordial than truth, since if truth is to be seen as disclosure or revelation, there must first of all be closure and concealment. The opaque, impenetrable 'earth' is the ground of that opening up of intelligibility which is 'world'. The conventional view – that truth is prior to falsehood, since it is only by virtue of the former that we can identify the latter – is dismissed out of hand. Yet we still need to ask how we can identify concealment in the first place without invoking some conception of truth.[39]

Yeats, Wilde, Sorel and their colleagues shift from truth as correspondence to truth as authenticity. A fidelity to fact gives way to a fidelity to self. Yet if the self is volatile and unstable, as it is for the Nietzschean Wilde, it is hard to know exactly what one is being faithful to. Today's truth is not yesterday's. Later, with the advent of postmodern thought, nothing will seem more fake than the authentic. In the meanwhile, however, we have works such as Arthur Miller's *A View from the Bridge*, which claims of its protagonist that he is not 'purely good' (measured by standards that are in some sense objective) but 'himself purely', as though to be oneself were unequivocally a virtue. In a morally relative world, what matters is less the nature of your commitment than the constancy with which you cling to it. To refuse to back down from your desire, even as you are driven by it to the extreme limit of death, becomes a new form of absolute value. What matters is going all the way, not the direction in which one is travelling. It is a formalistic case,[40] which, as we have seen, has reared its head in our own time in a Lacanian ethics of the Real. A demonic version of it is to be found in Herman Melville's Captain Ahab. It is an outlook appropriate to a democratic age, since you do not need to be a demi-god or an archduke to be unyielding. Besides, what matters to democratic politics is not just the content of a decision, which may turn out to be disastrous, but the fact that it is we who take it. The same spirit informs a Kantian ethics.

Traditional moral codes still have authority, but they are now at odds with a more existential type of ethics. What if the objectively good is not good for you? What if the need to be yourself forces you to flout moral orthodoxy? The Thomas More of Robert Bolt's play *A Man for All Seasons* acts in quasi-existentialist fashion in accordance with the law of his own being, not, like the historical More, in conformity to the law of God and his political duty. Jean Anouihl's Antigone suspects that she may be burying her brother purely for her own sake, not out of respect for the gods or the claims of kinship. The tragic protagonist is now anyone plucked from the street and pushed to her limit. In principle, there is nobody who is not capable of being a Leontes or a Medea. Behind this lurks the modernist prejudice that daily existence is irrevocably compromised, and that only some act of madness or violence – some stunning epiphany, absurdist gesture or shattering revelation, one which will itself be eventually absorbed into the soulless logic of the everyday– can disrupt its deadening routines. Only by pressing things to an extreme can they be forced to reveal their true nature, which generally turns out to be horrific. The fact that prudence and constraint may themselves require a certain moral strength is set aside.

A distinctive mark of modern tragedy, according to Hegel's *Aesthetics*, is a protagonist who is driven by an unflinching fidelity to his own selfhood. Since this one-sidedness is irreconcilable with the social whole, it is bound to result in his destruction. In similar vein, the Lacanian psychoanalyst Jacques-Alain Miller sees the tragic mode of existence as a matter of steadfast loyalty to a master signifier, one which lends meaning and consistency to one's life.[41] It is a typically modernist piece of ideology, as the fiction of Joseph Conrad illustrates. We are invited to admire Lord Jim's allegiance to an ideal of pure self-presence – to a vision of some act in which he might realise his selfhood whole and entire. If this is a phantasm for creatures like ourselves, enslaved as we are to time, chance and contingency, it is nonetheless an exalted one, as well as being part of the stuff of which empires are constructed. Better perhaps to be deluded and heroic than clear-eyed and commonplace.

Rather as truth itself is shot through with illusion, so illusion can reveal something of the truth. 'I was made to look at the convention that lurks in all truth,' observes the narrator of *Lord Jim*, 'and on the essential sincerity of falsehood.' Indeed, literary fiction itself is an example of an authentic lie – 'the truth disclosed in a moment of illusion', as the narrator describes his account of Jim's career. 'A man that is born,' comments the metaphysically minded merchant Stein, 'falls into a dream like a man who falls into the sea. If he tries to climb out into the air as inexperienced people endeavour to do, he drowns. . . . No, I tell you! The way is to the destructive element submit yourself, and with the exertions of your hands and feet in the water make the deep, deep sea keep you up.' Only by embracing the chimerical nature of the real can one survive. To try to escape it by scrambling into the upper air of true knowledge is to perish. Stein then reframes his advice in rather more banal, Hollywood-like terms: 'To follow the dream, and again to follow the dream . . .'

What distinguishes the case from off-the-peg American ideology is the ambiguous character of the dream itself, which devastates as well as inspires. The same is true of *The Great Gatsby*. '[Jim] is romantic – romantic', Stein comments. 'And that is very bad – very bad . . . Very good, too.' There is no flawless ideal or incontestable truth, but we will wither the moment we confess the fact. Like Conrad's own writing, the dream is at once vivid and evanescent, misty yet palpable. To be free of illusions, observes the narrator of *Lord Jim*, is to be respectable, safe and dull. Realism is bad for you. Even the unspeakable Kurtz of *Heart of Darkness* is supposed to win a degree of respect for the way he has peered so dauntlessly into the Dionysian abyss, in contrast to the dewy-eyed social reformers and hollow men of the middle-class suburbs. The novella ends with the narrator providing Kurtz's fiancée with a fiction from which she may reap consolation for the rest of her days.

If Conrad is a tragic author, it is among other things because life-lies are both destructive and essential. In his finest work, *Nostromo*, almost all honourable ideals are forms of sublimated selfishness, flimsy disguises for material interests. Public altruism is covertly in the service of private egoism. Nostromo himself, a chronic self-idealiser, is hollow to the core, an incarnate fiction who as his name suggests exists only in the approving gaze of his fellows. Yet those who renounce ideals are faithless materialists, who come to grief along with the fantasists they oppose. Martin Decoud sees the rallying cries of patriotism, liberty and social order as so many masks for material exploitation, a sound enough judgement in the novel's own view; but this Parisian dilettante is nevertheless left to die of his own disbelief. He harbours only one delusion, his love for Antonia; but he is conscious of its vacuity, which in this context is the nearest one can come to clear-sightedness. Dr Monygham is a misanthrope who has been stripped of all pious misconceptions about his fellow humans; but this may amount to no more than rationalising a personal failure, since he was broken by torture earlier in his career. The high-minded Gould declares that 'liberty, democracy, patriotism, government – all of them have a flavour of murder and folly'. Yet though social order may be ontologically groundless, it remains politically indispensable. With impeccable even-handedness, the ground is cut from beneath sceptic and idealist alike. Those like the veteran Italian republican Giorgio Viola who are gripped by myths of political liberation are as blind as the brutal opportunists (Sotillo, Montero) who live by power alone.

There is a similar ambiguity at work in Conrad's *The Secret Agent.* The everyday world is squalid and corrupt, but the anarchists who seek to transform it in the name of an ideal are either mad or malevolent. It is a choice between a seedy but stable English normality and a fascinating but repellent Continental nihilism. The reader is allowed nowhere else to stand. The truth is devastating, but false consciousness provides only a flimsy defence against it. Winnie Verloc, the long-suffering spouse of a child-killer, a woman encircled by espionage, terrorism, conspiracy and pornography, is of the opinion that life does not bear too much looking into. 'It's extraordinary how we go through life with eyes half shut, with dull ears, with dormant thoughts', muses Marlow in Conrad's *Lord Jim*. 'Perhaps it's just as well; and it may be that it is this very dullness that makes life to the incalculable majority so supportable and so welcome.' It is certainly true of McWhirr in Conrad's *Typhoon*, whose bovine lack of imagination gets him safely through a storm.

Winnie is one of the great regiment of folk for whom knowledge and felicity are mutually incompatible. Consciousness is more a matter of self-protection than self-awareness. The only authentic action she undertakes in the novel (burying a knife in her husband's chest) seems to spring like an emanation of the Real from some depth beneath her everyday experience, which is why, rather like Lord Jim's infamous jump from the *Patna*, it seems impossible for the narrative to present it directly. Moments of pure freedom or decision fall outside the frame of representation.

Sophocles' Oedipus is seized by what the Freudians would call epistemophilia, or a voracious drive for knowledge. It is his refusal to back down from exploring his own illicit origins that causes his downfall. His wife Jocasta, by contrast, has no such inconvenient passion. On the contrary, she believes that her husband's obduracy risks undermining the foundations of the symbolic order. If there is the desire to know, there is also the will to oblivion:

> Best live as best we may, from day to day.
> Nor need this mother-marrying frighten you;
> Many a man has dreamt as much. Such things
> Must be forgotten, if life is to be endured.

Incestuous thoughts are two a penny, and what keeps us afloat is a carefully cultivated amnesia. The same, as we have seen, is true of the political state. Jocasta believes in deliberately living a lie, or at least in wilfully suppressing the truth. In this respect she is an antique version of Winnie Verloc. Rather as Jocasta is both wife and mother to the same man, so Winnie acts the role of mother to her younger brother, who is blown to bits by a terrorist bomb. Like revolutionary violence, the scrambling of blood relations is an assault on the symbolic order and has a flavour of death about it.

Dramatic character is itself a fictional affair, and theatre itself ranks among the most fruitful of falsehoods. Shakespeare's drama is often to be found reflecting on its own theatricality, playing off illusions against realities that are themselves laced with fantasy, or stacking one imaginary world within another in a giddying *mise-en-abîme*. A play may announce itself as a dream, tale or comedy, anticipate its own comedic conclusion (*All's Well That Ends Well*) or allude to the gratuitous nature of its art (*Twelfth Night, or What You Will, As You Like It, Much Ado About Nothing*). Despite his interest in theatre, Hamlet, as we have seen already, is an indifferent actor, incapable of sticking to his script, too fretfully self-conscious to identify with his allotted part as avenger. Othello and Coriolanus, by contrast, are all too accomplished players, incapable of stepping out of their meticulously self-scripted roles for a spot of ironic self-reflection. Othello in particular, who (much to the disgust of the plain-speaking Iago) delivers his mouth-filling discourse as though he has been assiduously rehearsing it in the wings, has a thespian's eye for the finely burnished phrase and histrionic gesture. F.R. Leavis describes his suicide as 'a superb *coup de théâtre*'.[42]

Only through mask, riddle, charade, wordplay and role-playing might the crazed Lear be brought to his senses, along with the sorely distracted Gloucester. When truth itself has become fraudulent, only a homeopathic admixture of illusion, concocted by a conspiracy of fools and madmen, can hope to restore it. The hero's masquerade of madness in Luigi Pirandello's play *Henry IV* is a critique of what he regards as the lunacy of everyday life. The title *The Tempest* is mildly duplicitous, since the storm we witness as the play opens is instantly exposed as a work of art rather than an act of Nature. Like all genuine artefacts, Prospero's magic island is an illusion aware of its own lack of foundations, and the play will be over only when the audience recognise this fact by breaking into applause. When *Macbeth* looks for an image of ontological emptiness, it is to the theatre that it turns. Yet since the theatre is a matter of illusion to the second power, a semblance aware of its own seeming, it is able to reflect upon the nature of false consciousness rather than simply serving up one more example of it. Art is the place where the unfounded nature of human existence is able to confront itself. In this sense, it is both more and less real than the world in which it is set – a world which assumes that it has terra firma beneath its feet.

Perhaps the purest form of illusion is power. The despot is a sorcerer whose world is magically pliable to his merest whim. It is the theme of Calderón's *Life Is a Dream*, a play whose protagonist, Segismundo, shuttles between fantasy and reality before finally coming to recognise that to live authentically is to live ironically, aware of the fleeting, weightless nature of human affairs (not least of political sovereignty), and steadfast in the knowledge that those who pay homage to this fragility cannot be duped. To be truly disenchanted is to know that one's life is framed by fantasy, an insight which may then inspire you to temper your arrogance with a degree of compassion. It is thus that epistemology becomes an ethics. Once we confess that what we hold dear is perishable stuff which (in Segismundo's words) is ours only on account, we can be free of anxiety and acquisitiveness in order to live more fruitfully.

To live abundantly is to dwell in the shadow of death. One may contrast this clarity of vision with the mystified state of mind of Friedrich Schiller's Wallenstein, who like Othello clings to his self-deception to the end.

One thinks also of Henrik Ibsen's visionary idealists, who turn their back on various life-denying doctrines in the name of freedom, truth and joy. Yet, as we have seen, the Ibsenite ideal is always tainted. It is tarnished by the arrogance, abstraction, naivety, spiritual elitism, intractability, hot-headedness or evangelical self-righteousness of some of those who proclaim it. From Brand and Thomas Stockmann to Hedda Gabler and Hilde Wangel, a number of Ibsen's protagonists join the tradition of those from Antigone onwards who are driven to an extreme limit by an unyielding demand at the core of the self. It is a hunger for life deeply interwoven with *Thanatos*, or the death drive. If the actions of these small-town *Ubermenschen* have an aesthetic brio and panache about them, we are also made aware that the visionary is not always easy to distinguish from the rampant egoist, or the creative transgressor from the criminal one. The Stockmann of *An Enemy of the People* is courageously prepared to defend the truth *contra mundum*, but to do so he is ready to raze the whole rotten edifice of his community to the ground. In his view, the common people are animals and public opinion is inherently worthless. There is little conception in Ibsen of a corporate response to social ills. Instead, one must battle for the soul of a community for which one may feel little but contempt. Politics, as for many a modernist artist, is part of the problem rather than the solution.

A coupling of abstract idealism and hard-headed realism is a familiar feature of middle-class society. Marx objects not so much to middle-class ideals, which he sees for the most part as honourable enough, as to the fact that they exist in conditions which make them incapable of being realised. They are destined to sit cheek by jowl with an recalcitrant reality. The gap between ideal and reality is structural, not accidental. Romanticism and Utilitarianism, Marx observes, are sides of the same coin. It is just this contradictory coexistence that we find in Ibsen's theatre. Gregers Werle, the priggish, meddling reformer of *The Wild Duck*, succeeds in tearing a family apart in his stiff-necked pursuit of truth. What Werle himself terms an ideal, the more pragmatically minded Dr Relling calls a lie. The truth is a fetish which holds tyrannical sway over human flesh and blood. 'I've ruined my life for the sake of a fantasy', laments Vilhelm Fodal in *John Gabriel Borkman* (Act 2). Yet Relling himself is far from averse to peddling illusions, provided they are of a life-preservative kind. His objection to Werle is that he touts the sort of fictions that are likely to destroy men and women with their pitiless demands, rather than help these spiritually medi-ocre creatures to muddle through. So it is that he encourages Hjalmar Ekdal to believe that he has the makings of a great inventor, while at the same time convincing his dissolute companion Molvik that he is a demoniac rather than a drunk.

Relling, then, pits his common-or-garden life-lies against what he sees as Werle's death-dealing fantasies. In his view, Gregers' inflamed conscience is simply a more fastidious version of the sickness he sets out to cure, so that, rather like Hamlet, it is hard to know whether he represents a solution to the general malaise or a symptom of it. Perhaps Gregers' mission to deprive others of their opiate is simply his own form of life-lie. Untruth is built into the passion for truth. 'There comes a moment,' comments the Captain in August Strindberg's *Dance of Death*, 'when the ability to invent . . . ends. And then reality is revealed in all its nakedness' (Act 3). Yet what if such nakedness is simply another artifice? Werle's resoluteness commands some respect, but the idealist may be as eager to use others to achieve his ends as Ibsen's lawyers and manufacturers are ready to immolate their fellow citizens on the altar of their own self-interest. The visionary and the sceptic are also alike in belittling the common people's capacity for truth. Ironically, Relling resembles Werle in his demeaning view of the masses. Both men differ from prophets such as John Rosmer and Karsten Bernick who trust to the possibility of a general enlightenment. Truth, as for Nietzsche, may be death-dealing, but it can also emancipate, a fact which Nietzsche is far less ready to grant.

If truth is an ambivalent affair, it is not least because too many unsavoury secrets are waiting to come to light, especially when it comes to that cockpit of false consciousness, the family. From *Oedipus Tyrannus* to *Death of a Salesman*, the domestic hearth is a place where the truth is routinely suppressed. The traditional sites of tragic art – the battlefield, the noble household, the royal court – have a modern equivalent quite as awash with conflict, betrayal, despotism and revolt, one known as the bourgeois family. The fundamental unit of middle-class society is a place of mental torture and festering guilt, while the praises of domestic harmony and connubial bliss continue to be sung in the public sphere. The diseased ménage of *A Doll's House* is a case in point. 'We never told the truth for ten minutes in this house!' complains Biff Loman, the disenchanted truth-teller of Arthur Miller's *Death of a Salesman*. There is no need for devils and demi-gods for tragedy to flourish in a post-heroic age. On the contrary, the unspeakable can be found at the heart of one of its most revered institutions. This is one reason why the end of myth, or the erosion of the public sphere, does not herald the death of tragedy.

Ideals of truth and freedom, then, are more insistent than ever; yet they may turn out to be just as corrosive as the deceit they seek to expose. 'If truth is your absolute you will die,' warns a character in Sarah Kane's *Phaedra's Love*. Secrecy and self-interest lead to falsehood, but so too can a principled resistance to them. In any case, it is not hard to see the rhetoric of figures such as Thomas Stockmann as a sublimated version of the individualism of everyday life under capitalism. As a form of spiritual entrepreneurship, it reflects the very social order it takes to task. In these unbending moralists, middle-class society protests against some of the less palatable consequences of its own pursuit of freedom. In any case, there can be no simple opposition between radical ideal and degraded reality, not least because capitalism in Ibsen's Norway is still fresh and vigorous enough to appear as a revolutionary force. In fact, it is able to inspire poetic reveries of peace and prosperity in the more ardent of its apologists. So it is that the shipping magnate Karsten Bernick of *The Pillars of the Community* and the former banker John Gabriel Borkman speak of their plans for industrial development in the exalted tones of the visionary – of vast tracts of forest to be opened up and rich lodes of ore to be mined, while veins of metal buried deep in the earth 'reach out their curving, branching, beckoning arms' (Act 4). This is the heroic, world-transformative spirit of Goethe's Faust in his later entrepreneurial years, not of Dickens's Merdle or Zola's mine owners.

When it comes to fertile falsehoods, Ibsen's drama is particularly multi-layered. There is the lie of everyday life, in the sense of the swindle and subterfuge of middle-class society, but also the life-lie which can make this existence more or less tolerable. Then there is the ideal, which may prove either lethal, liberating or both. What if the honesty required to rebuild human lives from the ground up were itself fatal to human well-being? Ideals may turn out to be toxic fantasies, and thus as more sublime versions of the life-lie. None of this would be the case if I.A. Richards were right that, in tragedy, 'the mind does not shy away from anything, it does not protect itself with any illusion, it stands uncomforted, unintimidated, alone and self-reliant'.[43] Life-lie and ideal may coexist, as they do in the case of Borkman, who dreams of a glorious future yet falsely believes that he will be rehabilitated by those he has ruined. Or the ideal may be part truth and part falsehood. It may be true but tyrannical, righteous yet joyless, which is how Rebekka West sees Rosmer's schemes to enlighten his fellow citizens.

Ibsen's work raises a series of questions which echo throughout modern drama. Even if your cause is an illusion, is the tenacity with which you cling to it what really counts? Should you modify your demands for the sake for those who find them too exacting, or does an extremity of falsehood demand an equally immoderate remedy? Are you allowed to crush the consoling dreams of others if this is the only way to lay a foundation of truth beneath their feet, or is this the most baneful fantasy of all? 'It is probably as well to be undeceived,' remarks the narrator of Marilynne Robinson's *Housekeeping*, in a blunt statement of the dilemma, 'though perhaps it is not.' 'You and I and everyone else,' protests the Captain in Strindberg's *The Father*, 'have gone through life, unconsciously like children, stuffed full of fancies, ideals and illusions . . . And then we awoke; yes, maybe, but with our feet on the pillow, and the one who woke us was himself a sleepwalker' (Act 2, sc. 5). It is to Ibsen that the Captain's comment is generally thought to refer.

The characters of Ibsen's contemporary Anton Chekhov are often seen as spiritually derelict figures, adrift between past and future and sunk in sentimental illusion. Raymond Williams speaks of them, in *Drama from Ibsen to Brecht*, as engaged in an interlocking of illusions, rather than in anything one might call fruitful communication. Yet the judgement needs to be qualified. Uncle Vanya comments that 'when people have no real life, they live on their illusions', and there are indeed such figures in the plays: Toozenbach in *Three Sisters*, for example, whose attempt to lend meaning to his pointless existence by signing on for work at the local brick factory has much the same pathos as Davies' plans to obtain his papers from Sidcup in Harold Pinter's *The Caretaker*. There is a good deal of self-deception in parts of *Three Sisters*. Yet, as we have seen already, some of Chekhov's characters are wryly conscious of their own condition, and not many of them live by self-serving fictions in the manner of Ibsen's fantasy-mongers. These wastrels and eccentrics may indulge in the odd bout of wishful thinking, but few of them are prisoners of a life-lie. In any case, Chekhov's world is too crepuscular to accommodate the fierce light of a Brand or Borkman. Tragedy would be too stark a form for this sphere of half-lights and obliquities, the typical note of which is more self-castigation than self-deception.

Ivanov is full of self-disgust, while Trepliov of *The Seagull* accuses himself of drifting in a world of dreams. Astrov of

Uncle Vanya declares that his and his companions' situation is hopeless and that provincial life has poisoned their blood with its putrid vapours. Vershinin in *Three Sisters* sees happiness as beyond reach and suspects that he and his companions will all be forgotten, while Chebutykin wonders whether any of them actually exists in the first place. Liubov Andryeevna in *The Cherry Orchard* is a landowner well aware of her own ruinous extravagance. This is a social class present at its own decline. In fact, it shows a surprising degree of insight into its own moral bankruptcy, even if this brooding self-consciousness is also part of its sickness. The most common Chekhovian fiction, as with Trofimov of *The Cherry Orchard*, is a rousing exhortation to work; but, for all his specious rhetoric, Trofimov is well aware that civilised existence is built not simply on labour but on exploitation, and not many of those in the plays who wax lyrical about the virtues of toil are likely to be caught handling a spade.

Like all of J.M. Synge's plays, *The Playboy of the Western World* displays an extraordinary opulence of language; but unlike some of his other theatre pieces it is also a drama *about* words – about their power but also their impotence, their capacity to breed illusion but also to transfigure reality, their performative rather than representational function. Words in an impoverished nation cost you nothing, and the blarney with which Christy seeks to woo Pegeen Mike, as so often in Irish writing, can offer some meagre compensation for the boredom and barrenness of everyday life. The verbal exuberance of Synge's plays is at odds with the harshness of their content. The protagonists of the most famous Irish play of all time, *Waiting for Godot*, find relief from this desolate condition in the life-lie that a redeemer is at hand – an advent which, for all we know, might prove catastrophic were it to come about. In a later Irish play, Brian Friel's *Translations*, a member of an Irish-speaking community in Donegal has escaped from poverty and colonial repression into a dream of classical antiquity, proudly announcing that he about to marry Pallas Athene. Such fantasy is a recurrent theme in Irish drama, as Sean O'Casey's *Juno and the Paycock* would suggest.

Convinced that the timorous Christy has slain his own father, the villagers of Synge's play project their own fantasies on to this supposed parricide; yet the fiction turns out to be a productive one, as the hero assumes this false identity in earnest, speaking like a poet and displaying some surprising athletic prowess. It is not, then, simply a question (as Pegeen Mike puts it) of the conflict between a gallus (glorious) story and a dirty deed, but of the way in which myth can close the gap between the two by reshaping reality in its own image. Or, as Christy himself puts it, 'You're after making a mighty man of me this day by the power of a lie.' Since he has not in fact killed his father (which may also be true of Oedipus), he is the creature of a non-event; but the illusion takes on a degree of truth as the drama unfolds, so that by the end of the piece

Christy has thrust the patriarch symbolically into his grave in an act of filial defiance, allowing his father to be reborn as a friend and comrade. At the same time, he abandons the deluded bunch of dreamers among whom he has taken shelter – men and women who first remake him in the image of their own desire and then, seeing no further therapeutic use for him, cast him out.

The irony, however, is that the villagers really have turned Christy into a hero, though not by feeding him a false version of himself. It is when he comes to acknowledge this myth for what it is, recognising that the approval of this bunch of cowards, flatterers, bullies and manipulators isn't worth having, that he is able to find his meaning in himself alone, and in doing so to encounter his father on more equal terms. It is by turning his back on the heroising of his deed that Christy becomes a genuine hero. Now, indeed, he has a story to tell for the rest of his days, but it will not be the tall tale of slaying his father. It will rather be *this* fable – the narrative recounted by the play itself, the story of his adventures among these grasping, spineless, violent, sexually repressed men and women – 'of the villainy of Mayo and the fools that are here', as his father puts it, and to that extent a legend with a sound basis in social reality. An illusion has been converted into a life-yielding fiction, as the villagers' shabby behaviour helps to alchemise Christy into a more admirable young man than he was when he first stumbled into the shebeen.

Martin and Mary Doul, the blind beggars of Synge's *The Well of the Saints*, have their eyesight restored by a miracle; but having glimpsed something of the ugliness and villainy of their surroundings, not least each another's repulsive appearance, they decide to become sightless again. The key distinction is between being forced to live an illusion and actively choosing to do so. Those who emerge from blindness can see more clearly than the sighted: 'it's few sees anything but them is blind for a space', Martin observes. The pair now have a keener view of the ways in which others try to dupe them, a perception which is enough to make them yearn for darkness once more. 'Sight's a queer thing for upsetting a man', as Martin Doul muses. Even so, the couple are now able to incorporate a degree of knowledge into their elected ignorance. Conscious that they have been fed lies by those around them, they shake the dust of a duplicitous world from their heels in the manner of Christy Mahon, but in clear-eyed recognition of what they are renouncing. Like Oedipus, they opt for blindness because they have seen all too well.

Mary Tyrone, the drug-addicted wife and mother of Eugene O'Neill's *Long Day's Journey into Night*, is also self-deceived, though not in the wilful mode of the Douls. She refuses to confront either her own addiction or the illness of her son Edmund. Her husband, James Tyrone, is in denial about his own drunkenness – unlike his alcoholic son Edmund, who wonders aloud why anyone should want to see life as it really is if they could possibly avoid it. They live, he remarks, in a world where truth is untrue. The fog which shrouds the Tyrone residence is a rather too obtrusive symbol of concealment and false appearances and a flight into private fantasy.

A much inferior work is O'Neill's shapeless, verbose drama *The Iceman Cometh*, one of the few literary highpoints of which is the title itself. The salesman Theodore Hickey, a zealous, freshly converted acolyte of truth-telling, sets out to deprive the bums and barflies around him of their pipe dreams in the belief that to be free of false desire will bring them peace. Not even Larry Slade, a disillusioned ex-revolutionary turned professional misanthrope who scorns the idea of truth, and who is simply cooling his heels until death comes to claim him, is beyond the reach of Hickey's redemptive project, since his nihilism is in Hickey's view simply another life-lie. Disdainful of life yet reluctant to put an end to his own, this 'Barker for the Big Sleep' is merely rationalising his own fear and failure. 'You can let go of yourself at last,' Hickey exhorts his drinking cronies. 'Let yourself sink down to the bottom of the sea. Rest in peace. There's no farther you have to go. Not a single damned hope or dream left to nag you.' One or two of his companions, however, remain unconvinced. 'I've watched many cases of almost fatal teetotalism,' one of them remarks, 'but they all came out of it completely cured and as drunk as ever.'

Hickey, then, is the Iceman who prescribes a living death as the only cure for the chronically self-deluded. Only the dead or the utterly disinterested are free of fantasy. Yet this hope, too, turns out to be built on sand, since Hickey, consumed by guilt at the illusions his wife, Evelyn, cherishes about him, has killed her in order to free her from this false consciousness. To save her from himself, and in doing so to make amends for his own moral squalor, he shoots her through the head. The improbability of the situation belongs with the mediocrity of the play as a whole. Since Hickey's wife would never have awoken from her dreams while she was alive, it is best to ensure that she will never awaken at all. And since he ends her life in order to preserve her delusions to the end, as well as dispel them, Hickey has chalked up a double victory.

The spiritual death which Hickey promises his colleagues, then, turns out to have its source in a literal murder. Once the crime is revealed, however, his fellow drinkers seize on it as an excuse to retreat once more into their private myths, assured that Hickey is out of his mind (which may indeed be true). His campaign to put an end to their pipe dreams is simply an instance of his insanity. Rather than freeing them from their fantasies, then, he ends up reinforcing them. Since they refuse to buy the truth he hawks, he is no more successful a salesman than Arthur Miller's Willy Loman. The Iceman, too, ends up reaching desperately for bogus solace – the lie that he would never have harmed his wife, even though he has actually taken a gun to her. Like Larry Slade, his crusade against self-deception simply rationalises his own situation. The play does not allow for the possibility of a demystifying which might also be disinterested. There would seem no way of dismantling deceptions which does not count as one itself.

If the only options *The Iceman* offers its audience are nihilism and escapism, it is chiefly because the ideals of its characters are worthless. The dialectical vision of an Ibsen, in which an ideal may be both enslaving and emancipating, lies beyond the scope of his American successor, for whom vision has now lapsed into mere day-dream. Ibsen's flawed visionaries are out to destroy illusions in order to lay the foundation for truth and joy, whereas for Hickey it is death, not life, which lies beyond the prison-house of fantasy. Another such brutal truth-teller, who first appeared on the American stage at much the same time as O'Neill's protagonist, is Stanley Kowalski of Tennessee Williams's *A Streetcar Named Desire*, determined as he is to demolish the faux-genteel pretensions of the magnificently depicted Blanche DuBois. Blanche, who cannot bear to be seen in the plain light of day, is a purveyor of enchantment and a sworn adversary of realism. 'Yes, yes, magic!' she exclaims. 'I try to give that to people. I misrepresent things to them. I don't tell the truth. I tell what *ought* to be the truth.' Williams's *Cat On A Hot Tin Roof* is also awash with such reveries, as the Gothic horror show of the Pollitt family blind themselves to Big Daddy's terminal sickness, while Big Daddy himself is disgusted by the deceit with which he has been swaddled for forty years. His alcoholic son Brick, who maintains that 'mendacity is a system that we live in', hotly repudiates his own homosexuality, while the man he loves, Skipper, is able to acknowledge his desire for Brick only at the cost of destroying himself.

We have seen that Jacques-Alain Miller regards the tragic hero as loyal to a master signifier, while the subject of comedy identifies himself with the Lacanian *objet petit a* – the piece of trash, useless negativity or humble bit of the Real which up-ends all stable symbolic roles.[44] The trajectory of tragic theatre is often enough from the one to the other, as Oedipus, Lear or Othello are reduced to beggars or clowns, and the high-toned tragic vision is deflated by the farcical and grotesque. In Arthur Miller's *Death of a Salesman*, the confrontation between Willy Loman and his son Biff represents just such a stand-off between the comic and the tragic. 'Pop! I'm a dime a dozen, and so are you! . . . I'm nothing!' Biff shouts furiously to his father, who continues to measure himself by the American Dream. 'I am not a dime a dozen!' Willy flashes back, with deeply moving dignity. 'I am Willy Loman and you are Biff Loman!' Both characters are right: from the viewpoint of the labour market, the two men are indeed garbage, negligible, as exchangeable as coins, and thus comic in Jacques-Alain Miller's sense; yet Willy rebuffs his son by appealing to the sphere of ideology, for which the uniqueness of the individual is sacrosanct, and as such remains tragically loyal to a master signifier. His failure, but also his grandeur, lies in the fact that he cannot back down from this noble lie ('a phony dream', as Biff scathingly calls it) even as it is collapsing around his ears. It is what Arthur Miller himself calls his 'fanatic insistence on his self-conceived role'.[45] Scott Fitzgerald's *The Great Gatsby* speaks similarly of the colossal vitality of Gatsby's illusion, even though its consequences prove to be fatal.

One can see Loman's plight as a living disproval of Polonius's advice to Hamlet. What if being true to oneself means endorsing fake ideals and seeking to impose them on others, as Willy does with his wayward sons? What if your quest for identity means dying without ever having known who you were? What if you are forced to frame your desire for respect, commendable though it is, in terms that are morally worthless? Should one, then, like Biff, settle for the indifference of the Other and give up? Evade the issue altogether, like Willy's younger son Happy? Or, like Willy himself, continue to clamour for recognition even when this thrusts you into delusion and finally death? The irony of the play is that, through his inability to walk away, Loman represents a devastating critique of the very civilisation whose approval he demands. It is clearly not worthy of his commitment. Indeed, Miller himself sees his protagonist as haunted by the hollowness of the ideology in which he invests so deeply, and thus not as entirely self-deluded. In this sense, the play is less a tragedy of false consciousness than that of a man torn between illusion and reality, still clinging to his ego ideal while increasingly aware of its nullity. Another irony of the piece is that it shows up the sham of the American Dream while admiring certain values which belong to it, not least its hero's dogged self-belief. Eddie Carbone of Miller's *A View from the Bridge* also hurtles to his death in the grip of a false demand, but the play is moved by his refusal to settle for half in much the same way that *Salesman* commends (as well as criticises) Loman's doomed attempt to follow the dream. It is vital to be true to oneself, but what if that self is defined by a corrupt ethic of success or (as in Carbone's case) an archaic code of honour which scarcely deserves one's esteem?

Murder in the Cathedral is the only one of T.S. Eliot's plays in which spiritual truths can make contact with the common people. Indeed, there are connections between the two built in to the liturgical form of the drama, rather as priests, acolytes, choir and laity are united in the ritual of the Mass. By the end of the piece, even the timidly conventional Chorus has come to sense something of the significance of Thomas Becket's martyrdom, an event which might fructify in their own inconspicuous lives. In *The Family Reunion* and *The Cocktail Party*, by contrast, there can be no such commerce between those who are metaphysically in the know and those consigned to the outer darkness. Instead, we are presented with a hierarchy of levels of consciousness, with the spiritual cognoscenti at its apex, a number of bone-headed high society figures at its base, and a handful of characters in between who are dimly conscious that something momentous is taking its course but have no sure grasp of what it might be. This ranking within the play reflects one in the audience: in Eliot's view, there will be a select few in the auditorium with some glimmering of insight into a play's deeper meanings, along with those moral ground-lings who are not even aware that the characters are speaking blank verse.

The aim of the drama is by no means to bridge this gap. On the contrary, Eliot's theatre constitutes a space in which action and meaning – what we see on stage and the religious subtext to which it alludes – ostentatiously fail to intersect. Indeed, the plays take a perverse delight in this disconnection. As with Ibsen and Chekhov, most of the key events happen off-stage, since the naturalistic drawing-room setting cannot represent them directly. In this sense, the form of the drama acts as a critique of what can be shown and what cannot, drawing a line between everyday life and what transcends it. By keeping within the confines of naturalism, the plays draw ironic atten-tion to their own limits, suggesting that the kind of spiritual drama their author might like to produce is no longer possible in the soulless conditions of late modernity. In *The Cocktail Party*, metaphysical monologues are interrupted by the tele-phone, in a way which calls both spheres into satirical ques-tion. Everyday life is a bad joke, but so is the act of reaching beyond it: the martyrdom of the saintly Celia is a deliberately tasteless piece of *comédie noire*. The appearance of the Furies at the drawing-room window in *The Family Reunion* is another of Eliot's sly jests, as the dramatist throws up his hands in wry despair at the prospect of inserting such momentous matters as sin, guilt, punishment and atonement into the two-dimensional world of high society. The best one can do in *The Cocktail Party* by way of a spiritual counsellor is the psychiatrist Reilly, a secular priesthood for which Eliot's disdain is not hard to imagine. Like much in these plays, Reilly is a joke at his author's own expense.

All this, however, is not allowed to count too heavily against polite society. Everyday consciousness is bound to be false consciousness, and to expect more of it would be fruitlessly utopian. It is enough that a small coterie of men and women should see through the small talk and cocktails to a sphere of salvation and damnation. Spiritual values, not least if they are not to be vulgarised, must be insulated from common experience, even if this is where they are supposed to go to work. Both the realm of metaphysics and the world of Martinis are struck empty by their mutual separation – the one reduced to a few fitful intimations of eternity which can never become tangible, the other to a set of brittle social conventions. Eliot's Christian faith is not of an incarnational kind, whatever he may formally profess, and the forms of his drama reflect the fact. Yet though social manners may be idle, they must be preserved, since they shield the Hollow Men of Chelsea and Kensington from truths which might shatter them to the core. Human kind cannot bear much spiritual reality, and spiritual reality is not greatly enamoured of human kind. Were the truth to become apparent to the Edwards and Lavinias of this world, the cocktails would no longer circulate and the drawing-room chit chat would stammer to a halt. There is no call for an Ibsenite truth-teller in Mayfair. Each sphere, sacred and profane, is necessary in its own way; it is just that to mingle them would prove fatal to both. Eliot can thus send up high society while continuing to endorse it. A few lonely visionaries will abjure the world, but it is prudent for the rest of us to bow to its protocols in a spirit of ironic defeatism. Truth and illusion coexist, but they do not mix well. It is the opposite situation to Edward Albee's play *Who's Afraid of Virginia Woolf?*. 'Truth and illusion, George: you don't know the difference,' Martha accuses her husband, to which he replies 'No, but we must carry on as though we did.'

5

THE INCONSOLABLE

The liberal mind tends to be wary of outright confrontation, preferring instead to imagine a balance of opposing forces. 'Truth, in the great practical concerns of life,' writes John Stuart Mill in *On Liberty*, 'is so much a question of the reconciling and combining of opposites, that very few have minds sufficiently capacious and impartial to make the adjustment with an approach to correctness.'[1] It is the classic note of modern liberalism. Truth is many-sided, and partisanship can only distort it. The middle ground is the most prudent place to stand. Difference is to be celebrated, but conflict is generally undesirable. For the radical, by contrast, certain antagonisms are inevitable, and affirming difference may itself involve a struggle. The truth of situations may be one-sided: what is the middle ground between racism and anti-racism, and what judicious balance is to be struck between Jews and anti-Semites? Is it better to make peace with the fascists, seeking out some common ground, or try to defeat them? If the claim that women have been suppressed throughout history is partisan, is it not also true? To conciliate may be to defuse conflict in a way that suits one party more than another. Without justice there may be no relaxing of hostilities, and securing justice may mean having to fight for it. Besides, unity is not an inherent good. Nazi Germany provided an excellent example of this. There is also the question of who sets the terms on which a resolution is to be achieved.

'From the beginning, in all discussions of tragedy,' writes Helen Gardner, 'one note is always struck: that tragedy includes, or reconciles, or preserves in tension, contraries.'[2] Reconciliation, insist Miguel de Beistegui and Simon Sparks, is 'the fundamental demand of [tragic] thought'.[3] I.A. Richards, for whom tragedy is 'the greatest and the rarest thing in literature', sees it as a balance and reconciliation of opposites, as pity and terror achieve a delicate equipoise. The joy at the heart of the tragic experience, Richards considers, is not an indication that all's well with the world, or that justice exists somewhere, but that 'all is right here and now in the nervous system',[4] as the tragic work strikes a satisfying balance between our discordant impulses. The irony of this view of the tragic is hard to overstate. One might expect that the realist novel should end with an amicable settlement, since the form represents one of the supreme cultural achievements of a middle class increasingly at ease with the world. Yet it is odd to expect such harmony from the art-form which confronts us more than any other with loss and devastation, and which is supposed to do so without anodyne or false hope.

The essence of tragedy, Richards maintains, is that it forces us to live for a moment without the suppressions and sublimations which are our usual stock-in-trade. Yet even if this is true, it is doubtful that it is achieved by the device of equipoise. How could anyone plausibly argue that balance or reconciliation is the keynote of *Oedipus Tyrannus*, *King Lear*, *Phèdre* or *Rosmersholm*? Does Euripides' Pentheus make his peace with the world, and does concord reign at the end of Racine's *Andromache*? States of resolution, after all, are not easy to turn into spellbinding theatre. We tend to find discord more appealing than unity, which is one reason why tragic drama puts it centre-stage. No doubt there is a psychological impulse underlying this compulsion to unify, as well as an ideological one. Confronted with a set of fragments, the mind finds it hard to resist gathering them into one, as though gripped by some Kleinian fantasy of reparation, without pausing to ask whether they might not be better off left as they are.

It is true that many tragedies end on a tentative note of renewal, as Fortinbras stalks triumphantly on stage, Lear is laid mercifully to rest and Catherine and Heathcliff find refuge from the tempest of history in the grave. But these fitful glimpses of a less wretched form of existence must not be allowed to overshadow the heartbreak of the tragic action itself. Even when reconciliation is achieved, it would probably have been better if the events which make it necessary had not happened. When Walter Kaufmann claims that the value of tragedy lies in its 'refusal to let any comfort, faith, or joy deafen our ears to the tortured cries of our brethren', he does not mean to suggest that there is no solace in the art-form at all.[5] It is rather that for Iago to receive his comeuppance is no recompense for the death of Desdemona. Aristotle regards Euripides as the most tragic of the ancient Greek dramatists because he does not shrink from unreconciled endings.

In a current of tragic theory running from Schiller to Heidegger, we are assured that injuries can be healed, antagonisms overcome and death-dealing forces appeased. The apologists for an ascendant middle class are able to accommodate even tragedy within their dewy-eyed vision of progress. Not only to accommodate it, indeed, but to clamour like Nietzsche and Wagner for its rebirth in their own time. Ludwig Wittgenstein notes how out of sympathy he is with this way of seeing: in his world, he remarks in *Culture and Value*, 'hardship and conflict do not become something splendid but a *defect*'.[6] He assumes, in other words, that splendour is the hallmark of the tragic, and rejects it on those grounds. But there may be no need for the assumption in the first place.

The theory of tragedy which Wittgenstein rejects is particularly influential at the close of the eighteenth century and in the century which follows. It is not that tragedy has migrated from the stage to the study – though when it comes to Romantic tragedy, much of which is more poetry than performance, one recalls George Steiner's acerbic remark that rarely has a more distinguished group of authors produced a more dismal set of works.[7] It is rather that the form has some momentous theoretical work to accomplish, and as such is too vital to be confined to the theatre. 'Generalising about tragedy,' remarks Simon Goldhill of this corpus of work, 'takes tragedy from the sphere of literary genre and establishes it as a means to comprehend the self as a political, psychological, and religious subject. Tragedy is a route to the self-definition of modernity.'[8] It is the clash between freedom and necessity which most interests these coiners of a new concept known as the tragic – a notion, incidentally, quite alien to Aristotle, who in his dry, formalistic little treatise on poetics deals with tragedy as an artistic genre but not as a world-view, and judging by his ethical and political writings would have found the idea of a tragic vision unacceptable. That tragedy can unlock the conflict between fate and freedom is what a whole range of philosophers find most precious about it, so that tragic drama becomes an ethico-political affair as well as an aesthetic one.

One problem is that freely undertaken actions are bound to breed effects which are uncontrollable, and which may then come to confront the agent himself as a form of destiny. Not only may my free actions end up obstructing yours, but I may be a victim of them myself. So it is that freedom gives rise to servitude, a paradox that only a dialectical form of thought can grasp. From Sophocles' Oedipus to Ibsen's Karsten Bernick, Aeschylus's Orestes to Büchner's Danton, actions can return in alien guise to plague their performers. We forge the chains which bind us, willingly buckling on the harness of necessity in the manner of Aeschylus's Agamemnon. Liberty is its own most lethal adversary. In market societies, at least in Marx's judgement, this contradiction is the order of the day.

Alongside this problem runs another. In seeking to shape the world to its own ends, middle-class civilisation has evolved few more formidable instruments than science and technology; but what science has to tell us is that all material phenomena are governed by certain rigorous laws, and it is hard to see how human beings themselves can be exempt from this determinism. It follows that what allows them to rule over Nature also threatens to confiscate their freedom. Freedom must resort to prediction and calculation to achieve its goals, a project which may end up undermining it. To act freely is to assume that history is open-ended; but such action also requires a degree of determinate knowledge, and knowledge of this kind is hard to come by in an unpredictable world. As the philosopher John Macmurray summarises this Kantian dilemma: 'We can only know a determinate world; we can only act in an indeterminate world.'[9] To be free is to be self-determining, obeying only such laws as one gives oneself, and laws of this kind cannot be reduced to the regularities of physics. Yet if the moral and the material are divided spheres, humanity would seem to be ungrounded in anything beyond itself, so that we buy our liberty at the price of our homelessness. Nor can there be a material image of such freedom. What is claimed to be most definitive about human beings ('Freedom,' writes Friedrich Schelling, 'is the one principle on which everything is supported')[10] slips through the net of language, baffles representation and figures only as a mute epiphany or eloquent silence – as quicksilver, mercurial stuff which can be glimpsed out of the corner of one's eye but which vanishes when one tries to look at it straight. There can be no graven image of this quasi-divine capability.

The foundation of middle-class society – the free subject – would thus seem to be less of a bedrock than an abyss. This point of pure self-determination, sprung eternally from its own loins, is no thing at all but sheer negativity infinitely in excess of any determinate object. It is the source of our actions yet can be fully present in none of them. Philosophy, it would seem, can find no sure anchorage in this non-entity, and ends up clutching at empty air each time it seeks to nail it down. It is thus unable to think the enabling conditions of its own enterprise. Thought requires an absolute ground; yet if that ground is as unstable as subjectivity, it can be no more than an object of faith. For the subject to be made determinate, however, would be to rob it of its essence. To know the self is to undercut it, while not to know it means settling for a cipher, a black hole at the centre of modernity. Bourgeois Man would seem to be self-blinded at the very peak of his powers, a hubristic creature who undoes himself in the act of humanising the world around him.

For the school of Kant, then, there would seem to be a touch of tragedy about the everyday state of humanity, divided as it is between its phenomenal existence and the freedom or reason which eludes its conceptual grasp. The subject is everywhere free but everywhere in chains, living in divided and distinguished worlds, a slave in the sphere of Nature to laws from which it is absolved in the domain of spirit. It is a view not wholly remote from that of ancient Greek tragedy, for which men and women endowed with a limited degree of autonomy grapple in semi-darkness with forces over which they are incapable of exerting sovereignty, constrained to act but condemned to a knowledge which is always partial and precarious. 'In tragedy,' remarks Dennis Schmidt, 'one learns that the sway of the ethical is not commensurate with the horizon of the human.'[11] It is in the period that follows Kant's warning against too presumptuous a desire for knowledge, placing the metaphysical off-bounds to human reason, that Oedipus, with his hunger for a truth which will finally put out his eyes, stages a regular appearance in German philosophy. *Oedipus Tyrannus* is in its own way a Critique of Pure Reason.

Even so, there is a certain comfort to be reaped from Kant's reflections. In an essay of 1915, the phenomenologist Max

Scheler claims that resignation is the finest fruit of tragedy, as we find peace in the thought that no better world is possible. The realm of physical causality is indeed distinct from the kingdom of values; but in Scheler's view this frees us from false expectations that the world should behave in a morally commendable way.[12] Kant himself finds some solace in the faith that the gulf between Nature and spirit may be bridged by the aesthetic. The work of art is a material thing, and as such is an object of theoretical cognition; but in its unity and autonomy it behaves rather like a human subject. Besides, the art-work is both empirical and rational, sensory and intelligible, uniting Nature and spirit in this way as well. It is in art above all that the supersensible stages an appearance in the sensible. Kant's *Critique of Judgment* can thus find in the art-work a link between the world as an object of knowledge (the subject of the *Critique of Pure Reason*) and the moral or rational sphere which is the province of the *Critique of Practical Reason*.

What is little more than a thought-experiment or speculative hypothesis in Kant himself will then become a full-blown philosophical aesthetics in the work of some of his heirs. It is not long before the work of art is being hailed as the place where freedom and necessity are spontaneously at one. As a self-organising whole, the artefact is governed by a law or totality, and thus falls under the sway of necessity; but on closer inspection the law in question turns out to be nothing but the mutual articulation of the work's parts, each of which is free (in the sense of self-determining), but bases that freedom on its reciprocal relations with the others. Each aspect of the work is enriched by its interactions with the rest, and by conforming to the law of the whole is able freely to flourish. Poetic signs, like responsible citizens, pull together for the common good. The art-work is thus a political allegory as well as a thing of beauty, even if it remains aloof from affairs of state. 'Poetry,' declares Friedrich Schlegel, 'is republican speech: a speech which is its own law and end unto itself, one in which all the parts are free citizens and have the right to vote.'[13] Art offers us the vision of a unified political order, but a unity which works through its individual features rather than riding roughshod over them. It is the enemy of both anarchy and autocracy.

So it is that, in an age of revolution, art exemplifies a form of freedom which conforms to law rather than flouts it. In Gramscian terms, its authority is hegemonic rather than coercive. It allows each of its sensory particulars free expression, refusing to subject them to some rigid scheme, yet it is also a miracle of organic unity. If the dilemma of German Idealism is how to reconcile the freedom of the subject with its need to be well-founded, the work of art yields us a marvellously convenient lesson in how freedom and foundation may conspire together.

Since the art-work as a whole works in and through its concrete particulars, it is a model of sensuous rationality – of a form of reason which promises to unite the sensible and intelligible, finite and infinite, necessity and freedom, Nature and spirit. Art engages the senses, which is why it can transform men and women more deeply than any abstract doctrine; but it is not an unruly mob of sensations, akin to the *canaille* who stormed the Bastille, since its sensory contents are shaped from within by a coherent design. Reason itself is sensualised, so that it can remain in touch with human needs and feelings rather than sheering off into some bloodless rationalism. Freedom is objectivised, made to assume palpable form. Lurking beneath this model of the art-work, as beneath almost all aesthetic discourse, is a theological concept: that of the Incarnation or Word made flesh.

The harmony of freedom and necessity, the sensible and intelligible and so on are part of what is meant by beauty. But there is also the question of the sublime, which rather than reconciling sense and spirit represents the victory of the latter over the former. When we encounter some sublime object or event, we are conscious of a power which lies beyond our senses and shows up their limits. It is here above all that the question of aesthetics converges with the idea of the tragic. It is Kant whose *Critique of Judgment* shifts the aesthetic to the philosophical centre-ground and who is the great theorist of the sublime; yet, though he himself offers no explicit commentary on tragedy, Schiller, Schelling, Hölderlin, Nietzsche and other more minor talents are not slow to make the connection. In Kant's eyes, the sublime represents – among other things – the victory of the rational or supersensible self over the natural or empirical one. When we confront the possibility of annihilation in such stock-in-trade scenarios as storms at sea or dizzying mountain heights, we find within ourselves a power which rises imperturbably above such assaults on our physical existence, and which we know to be the free, noumenal or transcendent self. The subject is accordingly divided between its routine experience and a self which is not only infinitely higher or deeper, but which for some of Kant's more heretical disciples can actually be an object of experience. What is placed epistemologically off-bounds by the *maître* swims dimly into view for some of his acolytes.

Like tragedy, the sensation of the sublime is one of agreeable horror. In their blend of the fearful and exhilarating, both forms are brought into focus by the French Revolution – more precisely, in the ambivalent middle-class response it evokes. For some thinkers, the terrors of the event, rather like a spectacular shipwreck, can prove gratifying only when viewed from a prudent distance. As the idea of sublimity is given fresh life, so a new vision of the tragic springs up, and both emerge from a period of political tumult. Like the Revolution itself, the tragic and the sublime are both shattering and edifying, chastening and purifying, amplifying and diminishing. In the act of being cut brutally down to size, forcibly reminded of our frailty and mortality, we also enjoy a sense of exaltation, convinced that the human spirit is eternal and immune from harm. Both modes recall us to our finitude, turning their backs on the bourgeois dream of endless progress. Yet the fact that we are still alive, however fearful and overwhelmed, reminds us that our true home is with infinity.

In rather less grandiose terms, we are able to indulge the gratifications of the death drive in fictional form, assured that we cannot actually be destroyed and free to wreak some virtual vengeance on the forces that would hound us to death. True happiness, remarks Ludwig Wittgenstein, consists in being able to say 'I am safe, nothing can injure me *whatever* happens.'[14] It is only by taking arms against a sea of troubles that the tragic or sublime can teach us how insulated from such afflictions we are and only by a struggle against the natural world, however fruitless it may prove, that the spirit may flourish. In both cases, it is through suffering and heroic resistance that we come to feel the presence of certain implacable powers which refuse to give way, while knowing ourselves to be spiritually their equal or even their superior. In this sense, as in the formal structure of the work of art, constraint or necessity is the ground of freedom, not its opposite.

What is peculiar to tragic art is not a fusion of freedom and necessity, which on this theory is true of art in general. Its distinctiveness lies rather in the way it thematises this unity as part of its subject-matter. In this sense, tragedy is an instance of art reflecting upon itself. In his essay 'On the Sublime', Friedrich Schiller locates the conflict between spirit and senses, or the moral and physical, in the individual, who is then not hard to identify as the tragic hero.[15] The theoretical claims of his mentor Kant are thus converted into an existential condition, one which lends itself to theatrical performance in a way that the *Critique of Pure Reason* does not. Battling against overwhelming odds, the tragic protagonist becomes conscious of his power to withstand adversity. He is accordingly made sensible of his freedom – which is to say, of the rational self's autonomy from the material world, absolved as it is from the limits of Nature and necessity. The highest degree of moral consciousness, Schiller observes in his essay 'On the Tragic Art', can exist only in strife, and the deepest moral pleasure is always laced with pain. Both tragedy and the sublime are masochistic forms, as we delight in being stripped to nothing. Only against this backdrop can our true spiritual grandeur appear. To be nothing in particular is to be at one with infinity, since both states are indefinable. Both nullity and infinity slip through the net of language. In baffling our understanding, however, they yield us a negative knowledge of the superior faculty of reason, one which is sovereign over Nature. From this sublime vantage-point, we can suffer with all those who are ruined and desolate, even as we know ourselves to be safe from the calamities on which we gaze down from our seat among the Olympians. The tragic sublime involves both suffering and the transcendence of suffering.

There is another affinity between the two modes. Both proclaim that a world which seems in moral and physical disarray is in fact a realm of order and intelligibility. For both Hegel and Hölderlin, tragedy allows us to find meaning and rational necessity in events which appear to flout them. This is one of several ways in which it is a source of consolation. The workings of the cosmos must not be made wholly transparent, since this would be to dispel its mystery and sell the pass to an arid rationalism. Yet it must yield us certain intimations of order and providence all the same, if we are not to sell the pass in the opposite direction to the anarchists, atheists, sensualists and empiricists. Besides, those for whom the world lacks inherent meaning can easily fall prey to political disaffection. There is no harm in the odd philosopher speculating on the futility of human existence, but it is imprudent for the masses to do so. A faith that the universe makes sense must thus be linked with an insistence on the impenetrability of Being by reason, rather as the ancient Greeks strive to find justice and logic in the quixotic behaviour of the gods while preserving a dutiful sense of their otherness. Enlightenment rationalism, with its banishing of reverence and aversion to mystery, its wariness of the unknown and incalculable, must face the challenge of artistic modes which deal in precisely such sentiments. It is unwise to dispense with reverence and humility at times of revolutionary agitation.

Tragedy, then, strikes a balance between meaning and mystery. It must also find one between exuberance and restraint. Tragic joy and sublime exaltation capture something of the buoyant mood of a social class which is now actively making its own history; yet this class has good reason to be cautious of too reckless an overflow of high spirits, one which has wreaked political havoc in its time. Philosophy, not least the theory of tragedy, must therefore temper this enthusiasm with an insistence on the limits of human understanding and the inviolable nature of the moral law.

The idea of the tragic is born of a philosophical crisis as well as a political one. Kant decrees what philosophy can and cannot speak of, patrolling the frontiers of knowledge and excluding the metaphysical from its scope. There can be no more philosophical talk of the Almighty, the soul, the Absolute or the essence of things. Yet an age reeling from the shock waves of political upheaval still feels the need for such unimpeachable grounds, even if, as in the work of Hegel, you cast them in historicised form. Philosophy therefore retains supremacy over such inferior activities as art – not only inferior, indeed, but in Hegel's eyes distinctly *dépassé*, since in a fragmentary, unfathomably complex modern civilisation the work of art is no longer equal to the task of portraying the social totality. It is this function, so Hegel supposes, that it performed for the ancient Greeks. Besides, the growth of subjective freedom in the modern era is not easy to contain within classical aesthetic forms. Increasingly bereft of its traditional social, political and religious roles, art now looks to philosophy for its credentials, which is one reason for the rise of aesthetics.[16] It is convenient, then, that Hegel's own philosophy, being of a dialectical kind, already owes something to the spirit of tragedy.

The idea of the tragic emerges within a more general turn from philosophy to art, inspired among other things by Kant's chiding of the former's immoderate ambitions as well as by his *Critique of Judgment*; so that, in a lineage from Schelling, Hölderlin and Schopenhauer to Nietzsche, Heidegger and the early Georg Lukács, the poet comes to wrest pride of place from the philosopher. The aesthetic, spurned for the most part by Plato and passed over by much pre-Kantian thought, now offers to unseat the discourse that has displaced it. 'The tragic,' writes Simon Critchley, 'is the completion of philosophy after Kant.'[17] If philosophy is stumped by the problem of freedom and necessity, the tragic or aesthetic may come to its aid. And if the Absolute is no longer accessible to thought, it might always be the subject of aesthetic intuition instead, as it is for Friedrich Schelling and Arthur Schopenhauer.

What is at stake here is a curious reversal. Philosophy, Nietzsche announces, was born of the death of tragedy at the hands of such sterile rationalists as Socrates and Euripides, heralding the advent of that bloodless creature Theoretical Man. In his own work, the tragic conception of life is out to wreak its revenge on this lethal inheritance. Allan Megill points out that the *Birth of Tragedy* is an inverted version of Hegel's *Aesthetics*, elevating art over philosophy.[18] Having supposedly dealt tragedy its death blow, philosophy returns to the scene of the crime some centuries later, as well as to aesthetics in general. Not only is it now ready to learn from the tragic spirit, but by the time of Nietzsche, Heidegger, the early Lukács, Jacques Derrida and others, art is being granted supremacy over philosophy. Or, if not that, then a certain style of philosophising is becoming hard to distinguish from poetry. These, we may recall, are discourses between which Aristotle saw no discrepancy.

The aesthetic, then, is creeping closer to the centre of philosophical speculation. The philosophy of tragedy is in the act of becoming a tragic philosophy, a process that will be consummated in the work of Nietzsche. This also serves as a way of restoring the kind of metaphysical inquiry which Kant has placed under censure – an inquiry which in Nietzsche's *The Birth of Tragedy* is conducted in terms of myth and poetry. Since Nietzsche's tragic vision puts the very concept of philosophy into question, it would seem that the death of tragedy at the hands of philosophy will finally issue in the death of philosophy at the hands of tragedy. We are back to the Platonic battle between art and philosophy, but with the values of the two now reversed. Yet the victory of art remains precarious. For Theodor Adorno, the poet after Auschwitz is struck as dumb as his philosophical colleague.

If the strife between freedom and necessity cannot be put to rest rationally, it might always be resolved existentially. This is one reason why philosophy turns to art and theatre, even if there is something odd about appealing to a minor activity like stage tragedy to address problems common to humanity as a whole. Friedrich Schiller argues in his aesthetic writings that tragedy stages the revolt of freedom against fate only to demonstrate the essential unity of the two, and describes his own drama as tragedies of reconciliation.[19] The criminal Karl Moor in *The Robbers* hands himself voluntarily over to the law at the end of the play, and in doing so pays homage to the authority he has defied. The Marquis of Posa in *Don Carlos* dies a similarly self-sacrificial death, assured that his vision of political liberty will be vindicated in the future. In *Maria Stuart*, Maria meets her end magnificently, outdoing in regal dignity the Elizabeth who despatches her to her death. She, too, freely embraces her execution as an expiation for her crimes. If it is hard to realise one's freedom without risk of political disruption, it can at least survive in the form of an inner fortitude. There is, however, a more dubious form of internal liberty, as Schiller's Wallenstein demonstrates. Preserving his freedom of choice by refusing to take action until it is too late, he ends up surrendering his precious independence of spirit to those around him. It is as though Kant's noumenal subject, fearful that to act is to yield to necessity, undercuts his own freedom by failing to exercise it.

For Friedrich Schelling, reason alone is incapable of achieving a unity of freedom and necessity. The task of resolving them, then, must be delegated instead to aesthetic intuition, which can achieve an unmediated access to the Absolute.[20] A similar argument can be found in A.W. Schlegel's *Lectures on Philosophical Aesthetics*. If drama is the most satisfying form this resolution can take, it is because, as we have noted already, the concord between freedom and necessity, or practical and theoretical reason, can best be shown existentially; and it is in tragedy above all that this unity is revealed. By freely embracing his fate, bowing his neck to the yoke of destiny, the tragic protagonist acknowledges his defeat by the forces against which he revolts. Yet the spirit which allows him to do so transcends the fact of his failure, testifying to the immortal nature of freedom. If tragedy respects the act of revolt, it also pays homage to the powers which provoke it. In this sense, one might claim, it represents an astute hedging of one's political bets.

In Schelling's view, Oedipus's acceptance of responsibility for his illicit acts, despite the fact that he is actually guiltless, is at once a stooping to necessity and a sublime victory over it. To struggle in vain against an unjust authority is to prove oneself a worthy match for the forces that seek to bring you low. In Nietzschean phrase, it is a question of victorious defeat. To acquiesce in one's death demands at least as steadfast a will as that of the powers that seek to tear you apart. In accepting his downfall, the hero reveals a boundlessness in himself which is at one with the forces against which he struggles. They, too, for all their austere necessity, have their source in freedom and reason, and lie at the source of the hero's strength. Only a power which springs from beyond the protagonist's creaturely existence could allow him to yield that existence up. The hero thus bears witness to his freedom in the very act of renouncing it, buckling on the harness of necessity and acknowledging his actions as his own. By stretching himself voluntarily on the altar of death, he becomes at one with the Absolute, testifying to what finally transcends all weeping and lamentation. Tragic resignation rises above the very powers to which it seems to capitulate. The Absolute cannot manifest itself directly, but it can be glimpsed in the negation of the finite, which in the case of tragedy means the death of the protagonist.

The lesson, then, is that you cannot escape the portion the gods have allotted you, but you can actively appropriate it, make one's destiny one's decision, and in doing so demonstrate that the fate you have been assigned is not the final word. So it is that Shakespeare's Antony declares he will be 'A bridegroom in my death, and run into't / As to a lover's bed' (*Antony and Cleopatra*, Act 4, sc. 14). Claudio of *Measure for Measure* anticipates the sentiment almost word for word: 'If I must die, / I will encounter darkness as a bride, / And hug it in mine arms' (Act 3, sc. 1). In such instances of *amor fati*, *Eros* and *Thanatos*, erotic love and the obscene pleasures of the death drive, are hard to distinguish. There is a bitter-sweet, quasi-existentialist pleasure to be reaped from knowing that one is up against an invincible force, yet to wage war on it even so. Such an *acte gratuit*, with its cavalier way with consequences, taunts death to do its worst, trusting like the martyr that only by embracing one's nullity with the tenderness of a bridegroom might one find one's home in the infinite. It is death which provides the passage between the two. There is a reckless, devil-may-care defiance about the act of appropriating one's end, even if one knows that one's life is lodged deep in the bosom of the Absolute, and so cannot finally be lost.

The highest freedom is thus to abdicate one's freedom, so that tragedy represents loss and gain together. Both freedom and necessity, Schelling writes in his *Philosophy of Art*, 'are manifested [by the tragic form] in perfect indifference as simultaneously victorious and vanquished'.[21] Liberty can be achieved only through its negation, and self-fulfilment only by self-surrender. In this sense, tragedy is an exceptional case of a familiar condition – one, indeed, which lies at the very foundation of the *polis*. Only by yielding up their freedom to the community as a whole, as the Rousseau of *The Social Contract* argues, can individuals receive themselves back in an enriching exchange. Losing one's life in order to save it is a matter of maintaining political order, not simply an aspect of tragic art.

We have seen that the context in which the modern concept of tragedy emerges is the insurrection in France. From this perspective, it is both a progressive idea and a counter-revolutionary one. If it cherishes liberty, it also commends submission to authority. Freedom must be realised, but it is through loss, constraint, loyalty and self-dispossession that it blossoms. Schelling contrasts what he calls 'Greek reason', meaning one which respects a certain law, harmony and necessity, with the hubristic reason of his own politically turbulent age. If he is repelled by the prospect of freedom being conquered by necessity, he also finds little joy in the anarchic vision of necessity being eclipsed by freedom.[22] There are, then, three senses of the word 'tragic' at stake when it comes to the political earthquake which is the background of so much German Idealist thought. There is the everyday sense of 'terrible', 'appalling', as the tumbrils roll to the guillotine; there is tragedy as a metaphor of revolution, given that in neither case can there be a glorious birth without a violent breaking; and there is the philosophical sense of the term, for which liberty assumes its highest form in a voluntary deference to authority. Freedom and necessity are shown to be identical, as they are in the very form of the work of art.

There are other senses, too, in which the opposition between freedom and necessity is overcome. If freedom involves acting on desires which spring from the core of the self, then (since selfhood is not entirely a matter of choice) some of these passions will have a smack of the ineluctable about them. There is a sense in which we do not choose our most deep-seated commitments, which may then come to confront us with all the obduracy of fate. Antigone cannot help seeking to bury her brother, or Eddie Carbone salvaging his good name. It is not that they cease to be free agents; it is rather that they come to a point at which the contrast between freedom and necessity breaks down, as Nietzsche argues of the activity of the artist. There is no shortage of tragedies which turn on a will to freedom or fulfilment every bit as intractable as fate. And if freedom can have the coercive force of necessity, the opposite may be equally true. What looks like fate may simply be freedom in unfamiliar guise. If freedom rules the world in the form of Spirit, it must be the inner truth of the law to which the tragic hero bows the knee. What appears as a clash between fate and freedom, then, is in fact a collision between two different versions of the latter, and the apparent discord between them turns out to be baseless. Antagonisms are resolved – but only over the dead body of the hero. There is an echo of this argument as late as the writing of Albert Camus, who in an essay entitled 'On the Future of Tragedy' sees tragic art as staging a clash between a justified act of revolt and an indispensable framework of order.[23] Hubris for Camus is the great vice of humankind; yet only in the act of defiance do we confront the limits of our powers, exposing the boundaries we must not breach. Rebellion is secretly in the service of authority.

In dying, the hero shows that the powers which cause him to perish are secretly on his side. Behind this model of tragedy lies a theology of the Crucifixion, which Schelling and others project on to ancient Greek tragedy. (It is worth recalling that he, Hegel and Hölderlin all started out as seminarians, indeed as room-mates.) The law of the Father may seem brutal and barbaric in despatching Jesus to his death, but, because the law of the Father is the law of charity, there is no real opposition between law and love, or sovereignty and freedom. To call Jesus the Son of God is to claim that it is the Father's love which lies at the core of his identity, which means that his loving fidelity to God's command is itself a manifestation of the Father's grace. It is the Father himself who enables Jesus to accept failure, torture and death. The same is true on Calvary of the contrast between freedom and necessity. It is inevitable that Jesus dies on the cross – not in the sense that his end is predestined, but because juridical murder is the logical fate of those who speak out for justice and fellowship in a corrupt world. Yet Jesus's death, which takes a form reserved by the ancient Roman empire for political rebels, is also portrayed by the Gospel as one in which he freely (though by no means joyfully) acquiesces. Like many a tragic protagonist, he makes his destiny his choice. It is clear from his agony in Gethsemane that he does not want to die, but it would make no political or theological sense if he did not.

It is Friedrich Hölderlin who produces the most elaborate theory of the tragic in the annals of German Idealism, as well as the most esoteric.[24] The whole, Hölderlin argues, can be intuited only negatively, through the mutual conflict of its various parts – which is to say in human terms through the reality of individual suffering. Strife and opposition enhance one's sense of totality rather than obscuring it – so much so that the primordial integrity of the whole is felt most keenly when its various aspects are at their most isolated and individualised, since it is this which lends them their peculiar intensity. The totality becomes sensible of itself only when its individual parts pursue their mutually incompatible ends, and only through such individuation can it unfold its powers. It is at the price of suffering and division that Spirit can be triumphantly at one with itself. 'Reconciliation is in the midst of struggle,' Hölderlin comments, 'and everything that is separated finds itself again.'[25]

Tragedy, then, occurs at a point of maximum dissonance, as the intuition of a lost unity from which a fresh resolution will eventually spring. Antagonisms must be pressed to an extreme if they are to be overcome. Hölderlin's essay 'The Ground of *Empedocles*' sees the feud between individual and universal as focused in the figure of the tragic protagonist, who like Empedocles is torn apart in the struggle. Yet death and dissolution are an essential prelude to rebirth. Without absolute loss, no 'higher' resolution. The sublime totality cannot appear as such, but needs an earthly sign in order to do so; and this sign is nothing less than the ill-fated hero himself, who, when he is hacked savagely down to size, done to death and reduced to zero, can allow the radiance of the whole to shine forth without obstruction.[26] It is thus that nothing can become a signifier of all, as the finite bears witness to the infinite in the act of effacing itself. Only by offering one's body up to death can one be a pure medium of the Absolute.

The German aesthetician Friedrich Vischer argues much the same case in his *Aesthetics*. The tragic subject owes his grandeur to the Absolute, feeble though he may be in contrast to its glory. Yet it is precisely in this belittling of the human that the sublimity of the divine shines out all the more luminously, transfiguring the men and women who are its flawed vessels.[27] In similar vein, Karl Solger claims in his treatise on aesthetics that the Absolute or Idea cannot stage an appearance in itself, but is forced to assume some natural or material form; yet for it to submit to the constraints of Nature in this way is also the moment of its negation.[28] The Idea can thus be grasped only in negative terms, not least in the destruction of a figure (the tragic hero) which is bound to fall short of it. For Solger, however, there is some consolation to be reaped from this cleft between the actual and the ideal. What death reveals is that our mundane existence is no adequate medium for the eternal life for which we are destined. If the message of tragedy is doleful, it also hopeful.

'Tragedy, as the form in which existence appears at its most fragile,' Hölderlin writes, 'is simultaneously the form in which existence appears at its fullest.'[29] God is a *deus absconditus* who, as on Calvary, can manifest himself only in human weakness, appropriating for this purpose a sign (Jesus) he empties of meaning by bringing it to nothing. One is reminded of St Paul's remark that we bear our divine treasures in earthen vessels so as to testify all the more eloquently to the divine source of their splendour.[30] The more powerless we are, the more our moral victories must be ascribed to the work of the Almighty, who is thus glorified in our very infirmity. Hölderlin's Empedocles, however, refuses to submit to the *via negativa* of finitude, self-loss and one-sidedness, without which there is no true access to the Absolute. Reluctant to bow to time and material limit, he yearns instead for an immediate unity with the whole – an end he can achieve only by transcending his particularity in the act of self-slaughter. In his desire to be at one with Nature, he seeks a premature reconciliation with the world by hurling himself into Mount Etna.

For Hölderlin, humanity's relation to Nature can justly be described as tragic. Nature in itself is mute and has need of the creative word to communicate – which is to say that it cannot appear in its plenitude without the amanuensis of art. Yet any medium inserted between Nature and humanity is also bound to divorce the two, expelling human consciousness from the sphere with which it seeks to identify. The poetic word thus unites and divides at a stroke, as a site of both creation and destruction. The poet could only truly accomplish his task of lending Nature a tongue by surrendering his subjectivity and merging with his surroundings, in which case he would be struck as dumb as the mountains and oceans to which he seeks to give a voice.

Despite this irony, Hölderlin's abiding instinct is to conciliate. In an age of schism and revolt, we need to recapture the
Dionysian spirit which dissolves hostilities into one – a resolution which Hölderlin believed for a time to have found its
political apotheosis in the equality and fraternity of the French
Revolution. For him, as later for Nietzsche, the Dionysian
signifies a sense of primordial unity with everything that lives;
and though this Absolute continually takes the form of individual calamity, it transcends the misfortunes to which it gives
rise. This theory of tragedy, like that of most German Idealism,
is really a species of theodicy. Suffering, self-dispossession and
ruthless individualism are essential preludes to moral victory.
The guiding hand of *Geist* can be glimpsed in the apparent
anarchy of the spiritual marketplace. We are very far from the
world of Euripides, John Webster or Eugene O'Neill. Indeed, it
is significant that the German tragic theory of this period pays
relatively little attention to the theatre of Euripides, or for that
matter to the blood-spattered drama of Seneca, since neither
author offers its audience much in the way of edification.[31]

'Over and above mere fear and tragic sympathy,' writes
Hegel, 'we have ... the feeling of reconciliation.'[32] It is no
wonder that he was pained by the ending of Schiller's *Wallenstein*,
which seems to flout both divine and poetic justice. 'Horrible!'
he exclaims. 'Death triumphs over life! This is not tragic, but
awful!'[33] His own doctrine of tragedy, by contrast, holds that
discord and division will finally be subsumed into the unity

of what he calls ethical substance. In tragic art, as in history in general, the Absolute separates from itself, enters into self-opposition and descends, Christ-like, into the hellish realm of loss, futility and affliction; but it does so only as an essential condition of rising to loftier status. Drama is a particularly fitting medium for this dialectic, since, while epic deals largely in objective events, and lyric in subjective states of mind, the theatre is well placed to demonstrate the clash (as well as the concordance) between consciousness and historical reality. In Hegel's view, the ancient Greeks were able to achieve such an accord at an early stage in the evolution of World Spirit, which is now en route to reinventing it on a far more ambitious scale.

The rhythm of tragedy is thus at one with the inner structure of philosophy, which in Hegel's view is the dialectic. 'Philosophy,' remarks Miguel de Beistegui, 'is the site of the articulation of the tragic.'[34] As Peter Szondi points out, Hegel's *Phenomenology of Spirit* places the tragic at the nub of his thought[35] – though one might also claim that philosophy, as a reflection on what tragedy acts out in its more existential way, has a certain advantage over the art-form in raising it to self-consciousness. In a similar way, World Spirit requires Hegel's own thought to reach its consummation. The evolution of *Geist* assumes a tragic form, which is not to suggest that it meets with a sticky end. Dialectics is a matter of both antithesis and unity, loss and the surmounting of loss. 'The greatness of Spirit in history,' Hegel remarks, 'reveals itself primarily in sundering

and death, in sacrifice and in struggle.'[36] 'Contradiction, negation, sacrifice, and death,' remarks Dennis Schmidt, 'saturate
the life of the spirit so thoroughly and are so natural to it that
they define the very truth of the spirit . . .'[37] It is through a
process of aberration and misrecognition that the World Spirit
proceeds on its voyage towards its *telos*.[38] In the art of tragedy,
this history of blunders and blind alleys will finally yield us a
vision of eternal justice. It will also breed in us a sentiment more
edifying than shock, horror or sympathy, namely the serenity
which flows from a sense that the balance of the moral universe
has been retrimmed. In Hegel's eyes, this is quite as crucial to
tragedy as strife and contradiction. As with the sublime, we are
offered a fantasy of immortality. Individual lives may be ripped
to shreds, but Being itself remains blissfully invulnerable to
harm. We shall see a similar ecstatic victory over *Thanatos* in the
writing of Friedrich Nietzsche. Tragedy and sublimity are both
Janus-faced forms, allowing us to indulge and transcend the
death drive at the same time.

For Hegel, as for Hölderlin and Nietzsche, the infinite
appears only in negative guise, as a contrast with the finite, one-
sided nature of individual lives. Friedrich Vischer's *Aesthetics*
presses this belief a stage further: simply to exist as an individual
is to shatter the unity of the whole, and thus to incur a nameless
guilt.[39] Friedrich Hebbel advances a similar view: individuation
is the work of the Absolute itself, yet to exist as an individual is
to violate the self-identity of the whole.[40] In Hegel's view, the

characters of ancient Greek tragedy represent substantive ethical powers, moving in a world indifferent to accident or personal idiosyncrasy. As these figures collide, they create a momentary fissure in the true protagonist of the drama, which is Spirit or ethical substance itself. In the case of Creon and Antigone, both parties are justified in their demands, but each can establish its legitimacy only by annulling the claim of the other, and is therefore guilty, invalid and unjust. What is amiss is not the nature of a specific interest but the fact that it trespasses on the interests of others. The play itself has no need to bring these contending forces into balance, as *Antigone* conspicuously does not; but what we recognise in the ruin of the characters who represent them is the Absolute newly affirmed, as truth is born of partial knowledge. We can now attain a certain equanimity of soul, aware that struggle and adversity are essential to the upward trek of *Geist*. A secret rationality guides a history which might seem void of all purpose.

'In tragedy,' Hegel comments, 'that which is eternally substantive is triumphantly vindicated under the mode of reconciliation.'[41] It is just and rational that Creon and Antigone are both brought low, since this will repair the breach which Spirit has suffered. Momentarily fractured by a clash of forces, eternal justice is re-established in the downfall of the individual powers that disturb its repose. It is hard to see this as a persuasive account of Seneca's *Medea* or Middleton's *The Revenger's Tragedy*, not to speak of Brecht's *Mother Courage* or John Arden's *Sergeant*

Musgrave's Dance. Like most philosophers of tragedy, Hegel plucks a general theory from a limited range of works. If harmony can be restored, it is partly because – in Hegel's judgement – there are no irresolvable dilemmas in tragedy, as there clearly are in real life.[42] The drama of Pierre Corneille might be taken to confirm this claim. In *Cinna*, the title character is a traitor if he assassinates Augustus, but will lose the love of Emilia if he does not. Even so, the emperor's merciful forgiveness brings the play to a joyful conclusion. Don Rodrigo of *Le Cid* is forced to choose between avenging his father's death and his love for Chimena, while Chimena herself is torn between her love for Don Rodrigo and her filial obligations to her father, Don Gomez, whom Rodrigo has slain. In the end, the two lovers are reconciled. Yet it is not hard to imagine a very different ending in these cases or to find situations in art (Thomas Hardy springs to mind) in which you are likely to inflict potentially mortal damage on others whichever way you move. Arthur Schopenhauer writes of dramatic characters 'so situated with regard to each other that their position compels them, knowingly and with their eyes open, to do each other the greatest injury, without any of them being entirely in the wrong'.[43] Their eyes, however, may not be open, and the harm they inflict may be unintended. Hegel, by contrast, is a victim of the popular fallacy that where there is a problem there must also be a solution.

In Hegel's eyes, there is no great difference between tragedy and comedy when it comes to the business of reconciliation.

It is rather that comedy takes as its keynote what tragedy ends up with, namely a cheerful spirit. Even so, he does not turn his gaze from the slaughterhouse of history. On the contrary, his view of the human narrative – a volume of moral monstrosities which contains only the occasional page of happiness, and that largely confined to the private sphere –is decidedly grim. It is true that tragedy presses the breach in the unity of the Absolute only to a point at which it is still capable of being repaired, but it may create considerable havoc in doing so. Spirit does not cut a smooth path through negativity, but according to the Preface to the *Phenomenology* must 'tarry' with it, descending into hell rather than striving for instant resurrection. We must hold fast to death (of all things the most dreadful), Hegel admonishes us, with the whole of our strength.

So-called world-historical figures such as Caesar, Alexander and Napoleon bring devastation in their wake, trampling on the innocent. Yet this, too, is the work of Spirit in its march towards self-realisation. In any case, we should not be too soft-hearted about history's victims. Tragedy is too high-minded an affair to be distracted by run-of-the-mill sympathies. 'Your countrified cousin,' Hegel scoffs, 'is ready enough with compassion of this order.'[44] In this, at least, he and Friedrich Nietzsche see eye to eye. As we shall see in a moment, Nietzsche has not the slightest fellow-feeling for those who are butchered on stage, and neither for the most part does Hegel, who as A.C.

Bradley remarks in his *Lectures on Poetry* has strikingly little to say of human distress. In this, one might add, both thinkers are at one with Aristotle. For them, the pleasures of reconciliation take precedence over the discomfort of pity and fear. If we feel compassion at all, it is not for the characters themselves but for the ethical claims they represent. There is little place for simple misfortune in this exalted vision, and certainly none for sheer accident. Tragedy cannot be a matter of contingency. W.B. Yeats could see nothing in the least tragic about a car smash.

It is the conflict between the individual and universal which particularly concerns Hegel. It is this which needs to be resolved in a new form of human community, and tragedy has an ancillary role to play in constructing it. It is in the period of Idealism and Romanticism that the European bourgeoisie makes its bid to become a corporate, genuinely universal class; yet it is hard to reconcile this claim with its individualism. Marx sees a conflict between the excessively abstract citizen of the state and the excessively individualised subject of civil society. Modernity for Hegel must reconcile absolute and relative forms of ethical life, which is to say the universal domain of the political state and the sphere of individual needs and rights – of the family, the feminine, the body, civil society and the concrete particular. The *Oresteia*, he believes, achieves just such a rapprochement, as the domestic rights of kinship and blood alliance championed by the Furies are finally incorporated into the Athenian state. The fullest statement of the subject, however, is *Antigone*, in Hegel's view the most magnificent of all works of art, which he sees as staging a world-historical clash between the heroine's advocacy of the rights of blood, body, family, femininity, singularity and divine law on the one hand, and the masculinist, universal state of Creon on the other. The state is a more spiritually advanced formation than the domestic or private sphere, and preserving its authority takes precedence over individual lives. Only through their readiness to die in its defence can a people truly manifest its freedom. Yet the state cannot ride roughshod over civil society and the domestic sphere, and to this extent Antigone is in the right. Even so, her position is a partisan one, and thus can be fully endorsed no more than Creon's. The truth, Hegel maintains, lies in the whole. Yet this, ironically, is also a partisan standpoint, which it is always possible to deny. Marx, who holds that the truth is one-sided, will later do just that.

Goethe, for whom the idea of reconciliation is alien to the tragic sensibility, would seem to dissent from Hegel's theory of tragedy *avant la lettre*. Everything tragic, he remarks, rests on intractable opposition, and vanishes as soon as resolution becomes possible.[45] His own drama is famously resistant to the tragic spirit. Faust, his soul miraculously cleansed of the horrors he has witnessed, is finally transfigured by divine grace. If he is redeemed, it is because (in Lacanian idiom) he refuses to give way on his desire, which is for endless growth and infinite motion; yet the deathly lack associated with such desire is not allowed to undermine this project. *Iphigenia in Tauris* concludes with an affirmation of kindliness and hospitality. At the end of Goethe's *Egmont*, the shadow of death serves only to amplify the protagonist's zest for life. There can be no ultimate loss or defeat for this serene classical humanism. It is too ripe and replete for its composure to be truly shaken. Yet Goethe is not fundamentally at odds with Hegel and his colleagues. Both parties admire the kind of drama which ends on a conciliatory note. It is simply a question of whether you are prepared to call it tragedy or not.

History certainly does not disclose a rational design for Hegel's great rival Arthur Schopenhauer, who sees it rather as a squalid farce. It is the work of the malevolent Will, a blind impulse which the modern age might prefer to call desire, and as such is populated by 'constantly needy creatures who continue for a time merely by devouring one another, pass their existence in anxiety and want, and often endure terrible afflictions until they fall at last into the arms of death'.[46] This tawdry narrative of appetite, spiked ambitions and internecine warfare cannot even aspire to the status of tragedy. If it sets the scene for such high drama, we nonetheless succeed in bungling the opportunities for spiritual nobility with which it presents us. 'Our lives,' Schopenhauer observes, 'must contain all the woes of tragedy, and yet we cannot even assert the dignity of tragic characters, but, in the broad detail of life, are inevitably the foolish characters of a comedy.'[47] History is low burlesque rather than Attic grandeur. 'Nobody has the remotest idea why the whole tragic-comedy exists,' Schopenhauer remarks, 'for it has no spectators, and the actors themselves undergo endless worry with little and merely negative enjoyment.'[48] Purblind, insatiable desire is the driving force of the human tragicomedy, and men and women are its mere bearers or underlings, vehicles of its pointless self-reproduction.

'All *willing*,' Schopenhauer writes, 'springs from lack, from deficiency, and thus from suffering.'[49] The Will lies at the core of one's being, so that we can feel it on the inside of our bodies with incomparably greater immediacy than we can know anything else; yet it is also as alien and anonymous as the force that stirs the waves, and implacably indifferent to our well-being. Our desires are the last thing that we can call our own. It is as though we bear an inert, intolerable weight of meaninglessness inside ourselves as the very principle of our being, as though permanently pregnant with monsters. What is now fatally flawed is the very category of subjectivity itself, not just some perversion, division or estrangement of it. Nothing could be more obvious to Schopenhauer than the fact that it would be far better to call this whole pointless project off, and obvious for reasons that are by no means to be ascribed simply to some morose quirk of temperament. 'To enter at the age of five a cotton-spinning or other factory,' he comments, 'and from then on to sit there every day first from ten, then twelve, and finally fourteen hours, and perform the same mechanical work, is to purchase dearly the pleasures of drawing breath.'[50] What will release us from the prison-house of subjectivity is the aesthetic. In this supremely dispassionate condition, all desire drops away from us and we see into the heart of things, as though ushered into the presence of the Kantian *Ding-an-sich*. Dissolving for a precious moment into pure, will-less subjects of knowledge, we are able to shake off the servitude of the Will, give desire the slip and attain a condition of complete objectivity. One is reminded of some lines from Rainer Maria Rilke's poem 'Requiem':

> So free of curiosity your gaze
> Had become, so unpossessive, of such true
> Poverty, it had no desire even
> For you yourself; it wanted nothing: holy.

The most blessed state is to be at one with what we contemplate. The world can be liberated from the Will only by being aestheticised, a process in which the desiring subject dwindles to a vanishing-point of pure, self-oblivious insight, like one rapt before a magnificent painting or superb piece of sculpture. The only virtuous human being is the one who abnegates himself entirely, so that it is hard to say to whom this temporary triumph over need and rabid self-interest can be ascribed. It is as though Kant's aesthetic disinterestedness has now become a desperate strategy for survival; but it is also a pleasurable foretaste of death, as in divesting ourselves of our daily existence, stripping ourselves down to a state of pure negativity, we can experience the delights of the death drive while knowing that there is nothing left of us to be harmed by it.

The aesthetic is thus a foretaste of immortality. Like the psychopathic Barnardine of Shakespeare's *Measure for Measure*, one pre-empts one's death by committing spiritual suicide before it can lay a finger on you. Only through self-immolation can the subject be saved. We must contemplate the world as though we ourselves were not there to perceive it. In this liminal state of being, one in which we are both living and dead, moved and unmoved, we are able to look down on the madhouse of history with the supreme impassivity of the sublime, treating the human scene as a theatrical charade in which the shrieking and howling of human beings in torment is stilled to so much idle stage chatter. At the same time, we come to recognise the fictional status of the ego, as a minor contrivance of the immortal Will.

As we do so, distinctions between individuals drop away. The *principium individuationis* is unmasked for the fraud that it is, since the alien stuff at the centre of your identity is also what lies at the centre of mine, and selves may thus be empathetically exchanged. The aesthetic thus provides us with an ethics as well as an epistemology, as egoism gives way to mutual compassion. Ironically, it is because the subject is so detached, set above the bloodstained shambles of human history, that it is free to empathise with everything and everyone. Its empathy, so to speak, is a matter of indifference. Friedrich Nietzsche also regards the individual life as an illusion, as we shall see in a moment; but he rejoices in its literal destruction as Schopenhauer does not, and in doing so presses beyond the sphere of the ethical into a rather brutal form of metaphysics. Yet, though individual existence is baseless, it can give rise in Nietzsche's view to a magnificent mirage which draws a veil over the futility of the world, and in doing so renders it tolerable. It is this aesthetic spectacle which he calls the Apollonian. For Schopenhauer, by contrast, these outward shows are sheer vacuity. If the aesthetic justifies the horrors of existence for Nietzsche, it offers Schopenhauer a welcome escape-route from them. For Nietzsche, the essence of Being – the Dionysian – is to be affirmed; for Schopenhauer, the essence of Being is the rapacious Will, which is to be repudiated – though it is not clear how the act of doing so is not simply another exercise of it.

Schopenhauer's response to the tragicomedy of human existence takes the form of resignation. Only by renouncing the blind urge to exist can we live as we should: humbly, ungreedily, seized by infinite pity for the plight of our fellow creatures. If tragedy involves atonement, it is not for the hero's sins but for original sin, which is to say the crime of existing. Only by abnegating the Will can we overcome it. The price of this Pyrrhic victory, however, is alarmingly steep. It is nothing less than the extinction of subjectivity itself. We are a long way from tragic affirmation and transcendence. There is a feeling of exaltation, to be sure, but it no longer springs from a vision of peaceable coexistence, and certainly not from an insight into the essential rationality of the universe. It is born rather of a conviction that nothing ultimately matters. Tragedy does not aspire beyond everyday life to some sphere of eternal glory, but turns its back disdainfully on the whole fruitless business. There is no longer an effort to resolve the antinomies of freedom and necessity, since the former is no more than a sham. Nor is there any clamour for justice, since that, too, is a swindle. Heroic self-sacrifice is equally pointless, since both self and world are unworthy of our esteem, and one cannot sacrifice what one does not regard as valuable in the first place. Neither is there room here for an ethics of self-realisation, since the self is as mere spume on the wave of the Will.

Tragic art, then, is one way in which the Will rises to self-consciousness and confronts its own aimlessness. By presenting this mighty power as self-divided, we are able to perceive its worthlessness, and in doing so achieve a state of indifference akin to its own. It is we, the audience, who are superior to the sordid business on stage, not the stout-hearted figures of the drama who put us lesser mortals in the shade. No sooner has tragedy been honoured as a supreme revelation of truth, justice and freedom in the writings of Schiller, Schelling, Hölderlin, Hegel and their *confrères* than it is pressed by Schopenhauer into the service of nihilism. It will be left to Friedrich Nietzsche to reclaim it for the heroic virtues.

Before then, however, we have Søren Kierkegaard's reflections on the concept of the tragic. Tragedy for Kierkegaard is not the last word. It belongs to the ethical realm, a less sublime state of existence in his judgement than religious faith. The Kierkegaard of *Fear and Trembling* accordingly prizes Abraham over Agamemnon.[51] In the end, only faith can find a way of living with the contradictions which tragedy seeks to unlock. If they cannot be harmonised intellectually, they can be leashed together existentially. It is a mistake to assume that conflicts must either be defused or left unresolved. There is a third possibility, one upon which Kierkegaard seizes – namely, that oppositions which cannot be reconciled in theory may be welded provisionally together in the praxis of everyday existence.

If Schopenhauer praises tragedy as life-denying, Nietzsche insists that it was the theatre of Dionysus, along with their art in general, which allowed the ancient Greeks to rise above such a nihilistic vision. We have seen already that the tragic vision, like art in general, is in his view both life-enhancing and life-preservative. As he remarks in *The Twilight of the Idols*, art is not a question of pessimism but the answer to it. For the ancient Greeks, it is a prophylactic to shield us from the savagery of human existence, a noble deception without which we could scarcely survive. It is the medium by which we convert our Schopenhauerian nausea at the vanity of life into a set of spellbinding images. We are en route to the modernist platitude that the work of art invests a shapeless reality with a degree of order. Art for Nietzsche is an indispensable form of false consciousness. It is no longer a revelation of reality but a bulwark against it.

Yet the aesthetic is not simply illusion, since it also transports us to a higher state of consciousness. It is tonic as well as opiate. As Nietzsche argues in *The Will to Power*, it furnishes us with the primary means of rendering our existence possible, as the great seduction to life and the great stimulant of it. Without it, we might perish of the truth – the truth being among other things that there is no truth, at least as the metaphysicians have conceived of it. Tragedy is less catharsis than spiritual therapy. It is an immeasurably superior version of the vulgar illusions which, in Nietzsche's view, are rife in everyday existence, and to which the modern age might give the name of ideology. Superior though art may be, however, he is bold enough to reduce it to sheer semblance, thereby undercutting one of his own civilisation's most cherished values. In this sense, he deviates sharply from an Idealist tradition to which in other ways he remains indebted. His view of tragedy as balm for the world's woes, for example, sits easily enough with that tradition's impulse to reconcile.

If science and rationalism are tragedy's adversaries, it is largely because they reject its vision of the universe as a place of terror, chance, chaos and enigma, and thus see no need for edifying fictions to cloak the world's calamitous failure to make sense. Nietzsche's own faith in the need for such fantasises involves a certain perversity: you need cruelty and hardship if you are to take delight in the images which conceal it, rather as one might rejoice in a broken limb because of the pleasurable dreams induced by an anaesthetic. Beauty would seem to require an infrastructure of agony. A highly conventional aesthetics, for which art remains a matter of unity, harmony and sublimity, is coupled with an unflinchingly bleak account of the human condition. For Hegel, tragedy is rational and coherent because such is the fundamental nature of reality; for Nietzsche, tragedy presents us with harmonious images precisely because reality is neither rational nor coherent. Resolution in art is the fruit of a lack of resolution in life. If there is to be civilisation, there must also be barbarism. Nietzsche's theory of tragedy is therefore among other things a political allegory. The miserable condition of the masses is a *sine qua non* for the flourishing of an aesthetic elite. In fact, Nietzsche is brazen enough to insist that, for this purpose, the plight of the common people should be intensified, not alleviated.

In Lacanian terms, *The Birth of Tragedy* turns to the Imaginary (or sphere of Apollonian images) as a psychic defence against the obscenely pleasurable ravages of the Real, which Nietzsche names in this work the Dionysian and later the Will to Power.[52] Jacques Lacan's third realm, the Symbolic, is given short shrift in

Nietzsche's thought, since the advocate of the *Übermensch* does not stoop to such drearily conventional matters as the ethical or political content of tragic drama. Art in his view is not a cognitive form, and is all the more commendable for it. Tragedy is accordingly absolved from all commonplace conceptions of fear, guilt, punishment, justice and remorse, ideas more appropriate to suburbia than the stage.

If the Apollonian plays the role of Schopenhauer's representation, the Dionysian is the equivalent of his Will. It is, however, a far more ambivalent affair than the latter, mixing its lethal power with infinite exuberance. Like Lacanian *jouissance*, it is a blend of *Eros* and *Thanatos*. Yet Apollo and Dionysus are interdependent as well as mutually at odds. For one thing, the Dionysian gives rise to its own Apollonian self-dissembling, rather as both the ego and superego in Freud's view derive their power from the unruly id. The cosmos itself is in Nietzsche's eyes a Dionysian artist which continually engenders seductive images, so that deception is built into its very structure. For another thing, if the Apollonian is an effect of the Dionysian, then it contains a trace of the latter rather than camouflaging it altogether, rather as dreams for Sigmund Freud reveal in suitably gentrified form something of the anarchic truth of the unconscious. It is in fantasy that the Real becomes manifest. Besides, the Dionysian has need of the unity and self-discipline of the Apollonian, rather as the *Übermensch* vanquishes the chaos of his everyday self by hammering it into aesthetically gratifying shape. So it is that Dionysus comes to speak the language of Apollo, and Apollo the idiom of Dionysus. From the standpoint of the spectator, who is both deluded and discerning, blinded and perspicacious, the two spheres are not to be distinguished.

The Apollonian may draw a veil over the Dionysian, but it also allows us insight into its fathomless wisdom. In the sphere of the Apollonian, we stand for a blessed moment outside time, change and conflict; in the realm of Dionysus, strife and turmoil are never-ending. In one sense, the truth of the world is mutability, which tragedy used to lament but which Nietzsche celebrates, while in another sense nothing fundamentally alters. Bloodshed and brutality are constant, but assume a myriad of different forms. Mortal injury and mutual antagonism are constitutive of Being itself. This is why, *pace* Hegel, there can be no fundamental reconciliation in existence itself, and only an illusory one in the art to which it gives birth.

The Apollonian sublimates the terrors of the Dionysian, refining its raptures and imposing order on its eternal chaos. It also imposes order on the self, duping us with the fiction that we are unified agents and thus allowing us to take constructive action. Otherwise, we would find ourselves paralysed by the grisly chronicle of non-sense, self-ravishment and psychopathology that goes by the name of human history. In Freud's view, the ego performs a similar role in relation to the id. Non-meaning is thus recuperated for meaning, as Dionysus is transformed from a drunk to a dreamer. It is this which Nietzsche has in mind when he claims that the universe can be justified only aesthetically. For Schopenhauer, by contrast, it is the distancing lens of the aesthetic which allows us to recognise that the world cannot be justified at all.

It is the unperturbed gaze of the spectator, not the agonies of the characters on stage, which for Nietzsche lends tragedy its peerless value. As witnesses to the tragic action we can cheat on the death drive at the very moment we yield ourselves deliriously up to it, savouring our infantile fantasies of eternal life. At the same time, transported like the Schopenhauerian spectator into timeless, will-less, placeless centres of pure contemplation, we come to acknowledge that the ugly and misshapen are indispensable aspects of the mighty cosmic game, to be affirmed along with its more benign features. Tragedy, once again, is a form of theodicy: there can be no bliss without pain, no flourishing without withering, no supremacy without self-mutilation. Affliction lies at the root of all authentic art. The tragic artist actively seeks out suffering, affirming all that is questionable and terrible in human existence. Tragedy is the sweetest cruelty. The more life deploys its most formidable weapons against you, the more piously one should pay it homage. Pain and self-repression are for Nietzsche an essential prelude to the advent of the *Übermensch*, which is one reason why they are not to be repudiated. There is a full-blooded teleology at work here. Yet present adversity is not simply a prologue to future heroism. Nietzsche also displays a gruesome relish for it here and now. If Hegel takes a demeaning view of human hardship, Nietzsche greets it with acclaim. 'The path to one's own heaven,' he observes in *The Joyful Wisdom*, 'always leads through the voluptuousness of one's own hell.'[53]

Among its other benefits, suffering plays a formative role in the building of character, which is one reason why Nietzsche displays such contempt for the womanish sentiments of pity, fear and compassion. 'To consider distress of all kinds as an objection,' he scoffs, 'as something that must be abolished, is the *naiserie par excellence*.'[54] There is a fierce joy to be reaped from seeing men and women torn to pieces. Our distress at the anguish of the tragic hero is outweighed by our bliss at the sight of his annihilation. The ancients, Nietzsche claims, saw making others suffer as an enchantment of the first order, and knew no tastier spice to offer the gods then the pleasures of cruelty. With the reckless self-abandonment of a potlatch ceremony, the playful, self-delighting, supremely pointless, superabundant Dionysian spirit willingly sacrifices even its highest types, in the jubilant assurance that even more splendid specimens will eventually happen along.

'It is joy that is tragic,' comments Gilles Deleuze, a faithful follower of his master.[55] 'Tragedy must be a joy to the man who dies', declares Augusta Gregory,[56] a sentiment which might have come as something of a surprise to Marlowe's Faustus or Goethe's Werther. The tragic hero, Nietzsche writes, 'the highest manifestation of the will, is negated for our pleasure, because he is only a phenomenon, and because the eternal life of the will is not affected by his annihilation'.[57] What the hero's downfall reveals is the indestructible nature of Being or Becoming itself, which is as indifferent as the Schopenhauerian Will to any of its own passing manifestations, and so unfathomably fecund that it can afford to offer up to death any number of the profuse life-forms to which it gives rise.

Nietzsche is perhaps the most eloquent scourge of Christianity of the modern era. He sees it as a morbid, life-denying cult which views suffering as redemptive. The choice the age must make, in his own swashbuckling phrase, is one between Dionysus and the Crucified. All the same, the ascetic Christian ideal is not simply to be spurned. By investing pain and hardship with a meaning, however specious, it has served in its day to preserve human existence from a death-dealing nihilism. It is thus that life cunningly promotes itself by means of its own denial. Self-loathing and self-torment have played their part in sustaining the species. Yet the truth is that it is Nietzsche who sings the praises of affliction, and the Christianity he despises which regards it as an evil. Slavoj Žižek is mistaken to claim that Nietzsche is close to Christianity in his 'full acceptance of suffering and pain as the only way to redemption'.[58] The truth is that Nietzsche has a positive view of suffering, whereas the New Testament does not. At no point in the Gospel does Jesus counsel the sick to resign themselves to their condition. On the contrary, he seems to regard their blindness, lameness or madness as the handiwork of Satan, and devotes much of his time to curing them. The thought of his own impending agony on the cross throws him into a panic in the Garden of Gethsemane. Suffering in Nietzsche's view must be affirmed in order to enjoy an abundance of life, whereas for the New Testament it is obvious that sickness and abundance of life are incompatible. If pain and hardship prove unavoidable, and one is able to pluck something positive from them, well and good. Such moral alchemy is a feature of many a tragic action. But it would be preferable if value could be created in some less repugnant way. That good may spring from evil is tragic in two different senses. It may be a description of tragedy itself for those who regard it as life-affirming; or it may be tragic in the sense that there is something warped about a world in which such a steep price must be paid for happiness. The New Testament, for which what is awry with the world is known as sin or lack of love, belongs to the latter camp.

In Nietzsche's view, the two principles of Apollo and Dionysus only occasionally achieve a degree of equilibrium. The allurements of the Apollonian are strictly ephemeral. It represents the sphere of the individual, whereas the Dionysian dissolves all such particularity into the ceaseless flow of Becoming. What is at stake in the strife between them, then, is not only a clash between redemptive illusion and cheerless reality, but a contradiction between the individual and universal, as it is in the case of Hegel. In Nietzsche's eyes, however, this is not the thorniest of problems to resolve, since the individual is no more than a fiction in the first place. Its dissolution into the Whole is a blissful affair, not a matter of painful self-dispossession as it is for the martyr. The martyr donates his or her death as a gift to others, but there is no such moral or political dimension to Nietzsche's tragic thought. Self-giving does not rank high on his ethical agenda. What is painful is not the surrender of the self, since it is of no great value in the first place, but the process of individuation by which it emerges into being.

To revel in the horrors of human existence is to scorn a banal middle-class progressivism, but it is also to renounce all faint-hearted nihilism. The tragic spirit is an affront to the social reformists, but it also refuses to promote a pessimism which might infect the masses. One is able to experience an ecstasy beyond the reach of the average citizen, while having the courage to pay a price for this rapture which is equally beyond his grasp. Nietzsche can thus avoid the gloom of a Schopenhauer without selling the pass to a brittle optimism, and it is the concept of tragedy which allows him to do so. 'I have the right to understand myself as the first tragic philosopher,' he declares in *Ecce Homo*, 'that is, the most extreme opposite and antipode of a pessimistic philosopher.'[59] We have seen that, in the figure of Socrates, philosophy was supposedly born of the death of tragedy; now, in the person of Nietzsche, philosophy returns to this origin and proclaims the superiority of the tragic vision to its own style of knowledge. If this is itself a theoretical insight, it belongs to a form of thought which proudly announces its own passing. It is true that Nietzsche continues to call himself a philosopher, as will Heidegger, Jacques Derrida and a series of other anti-metaphysicians who follow in his footsteps; but as the barriers between poetry and philosophy are decisively breached, the term no longer means quite what it did for Plato and Kant.

As an astonishingly avant-garde thinker, Nietzsche is prepared to embrace scepticism, relativism, perspectivism and perpetual turmoil, cheerfully abandoning firm foundations and metaphysical absolutes. Yet all this is compatible with celebrating the traditional patrician values of hardiness and heroic self-mastery, along with a virile readiness to confront the unspeakable in the gleeful knowledge that it can never bring you low. A radical epistemology is pressed into the service of a reactionary politics. If the self, like the world in general, is formless stuff, then one must hammer it vigorously into shape, a project that requires the austere self-discipline of a military-style elite. It is an enterprise which signals the rebirth not simply of tragic art but of a tragic culture – one which, in turning from reason to myth, science to symbolism, rejects the rationalist delusion that mere cognition can penetrate the mystery of Being and heal the eternal wound of existence. In the teeth of science, equality, democracy, feminism, socialist revolution and other such contemptible symptoms of modern-day decadence, we must return to the art which says Yes to all things, however pernicious they may appear. A tragic culture would be one of cruelty and hierarchy, serenity and high spirits, delight in dominion and a reckless generosity of the heart, the magnanimity of the strong and the crushing of the weak. 'Back to tragedy!' has a perverse ring to it as a slogan, but not if one is thinking of spiritual splendour rather than war or genocide. This, generally speaking, the philosophers of tragedy have found little difficulty in doing.

Martin Heidegger is another for whom the return of the gods, the recrudescence of myth and the rebirth of the tragic will prove the only salvation for an age blighted by rationalism and technology. In the face of this dreary regime, one as self-blinded as Oedipus himself and quite as destructive in its lust for knowledge, ancient Greek tragedy for the later Heidegger evokes the fundamental strangeness of humanity, its openness to fate, the poetry of its existence and the unfathomable abyss of Being, of which the tragic is the supreme revelation.[60] Indeed, tragedy in Heidegger's view is the most profound of philosophical reflections, presenting us with an image of Man as dangerous, violent, fated, homeless and uncanny.

Yet Heidegger is writing at the end of a tradition, whatever his forlorn hopes for the future. In the late modern era, a positive estimation of the tragic will no longer pass unchallenged. A good many thinkers, to be sure, continue to extol art in general, and tragedy in particular, as a supreme form of reconciliation. It would be hard to surpass the extravagant praise heaped on the idea of the tragic in Georg Lukács's early essay 'The Metaphysics of Tragedy', for which tragedy looms up as a mightier phenomenon than history itself. As an epiphany of ultimate truth, it is the tragic vision alone which instils meaning into human existence. In moments of tragic crisis we are granted the privilege of a pure experience of selfhood, shorn of all empirical or psychological accidents. Tragic art is no less than the self-disclosure of Being itself, 'the becoming real of the concrete, essential nature of man',[61] the pinnacle of human endeavour and an occasion for mystical ecstasy. It is no wonder that in the tracks of Nietzsche and Heidegger, Lukács looks forward eagerly to its rebirth.

Other twentieth-century authors strike a similar note. 'Only in the realm of Praising should Lament walk', writes Rilke in his *Sonnet to Orpheus*, linking suffering and jubilation in Nietzschean style. The novelist Aldous Huxley argues that tragedy is too precious to be allowed to perish,[62] while the critic Kenneth Burke claims in his *Counter-Statement* that, though tragic drama itself may be dead, the tragic spirit lives on.[63] That it survives is assumed to be a source of value. For Joseph Wood Krutch, tragedy 'reconciles man to his woes', revealing an unruffled assurance in the nobility of the human spirit which no spectacle of suffering can impair. Instead, 'we must be glad and are glad that Juliet dies and glad that Lear is turned out into the storm'.[64] Oedipus's death strikes us as trifling in contrast to the greatness of soul it manifests. For Krutch, as for a whole lineage of blandly sanitising theorists, tragedy represents 'a way of looking at life by virtue of which it is robbed of its pain'.[65] Its purpose is to wring some joy out of existence by exploiting the reality of human wretchedness. Curiously, he then proceeds to undercut his own case by confessing that it is no more than a consoling fiction.

'It is not as though tragedy does not have a downside', another critic informs us without a breath of irony, as though after singing its praises he has just managed to recall that it deals in death and devastation.[66] The playwright Arthur Miller holds the startling opinion that tragedy is a more optimistic genre than comedy, confirming what he calls 'the onlooker's brightest opinions of the human animal'.[67] Behind the actions of the tragic hero lies a faith in the perfectibility of human-kind. Tragedy must trade in hope, since if the protagonist cannot claim victory over the powers he confronts, we are offered no more than pathos and pessimism. It is not a view which sits easily with Miller's own drama.

From classical antiquity to the American New Criticism, the doctrine of the unified work of art, resolving its parts into an integrated whole, has proved astonishingly tenacious. Remarkably, it is only in the early decades of the twentieth century, with the outbreak of the European avant-gardes, that this dogma is disputed on any sizeable scale. The idea of dissonance will now set the tone, of which the finest theorist is Heidegger's great adversary Theodor Adorno. Writing in the shadow of Auschwitz, Adorno suspects that tragedy, by investing human suffering with a shapely form, threatens to betray it. In foisting sense upon the senseless, it can only succeed in diminishing its horror.[68] A later, more equivocal commentator holds that 'it is equally perilous to find and not to find meaning in suffering'.[69] Nor can there be any final reconciliation of powers for the Freud to whom Adorno is so indebted. *Eros* may strike a pact with *Thanatos*, the pleasure principle with the reality principle, but they will never peaceably coexist. The human subject is split rather than self-identical. There can be no decisive victory over the cataclysm of infancy. We must simply live with its consequences as best we can. Civilisation is less an antidote to tragedy than an example of it.

The philosopher Georg Simmel strikes an equally chastening note in his essay 'On the Concept and Tragedy of Culture', claiming that though culture promises a harmonious synthesis between subject and object, the human spirit continues to be unappeased. The objects it fashions achieve a life of their own which then, as in Marx's theory of alienation, return to subjugate their creators. Tragedy is essentially reification. The forms in which life fulfils itself also betray it in their inert objectivity. Civilisation is self-subverting, undone by its own inner contradictions. Self-realisation inevitably capsizes into self-loss. 'Even in its first moments of existence,' Simmel complains, 'culture carries something within itself which, as if by an intrinsic fate, is determined to block, to burden, to obscure and divide its innermost purpose.'[70]

As the twentieth century unfolds, then, there is a growing chorus of voices which question the affirmative nature of tragedy. For Oswald Spengler's *The Decline of the West*, the art-form signifies not heroic glory but the irreversible nature of temporal development and the inevitability of cultural decline. In *The Star of Redemption*, Franz Rosenzweig is sceptical of what he regards as the tragic ideal of living by the Absolute, an achievement which is possible only for the saint.[71] For the Walter Benjamin of *The Origin of German Tragic Drama*, ancient Greek tragedy ends in a resolution of sorts, but of a notably provisional, problematic kind; while the German *Trauerspiel* with which his study deals, plagued by a Lutheran sense of the vanity of the world, knows no such redemptive closure. *Trauerspiel* promotes a melancholic rather than exalted disposition in its audience, admonishing them that happiness is the preserve of the afterlife. Benjamin's colleague Bertolt Brecht finds in the notion of tragic fate a ruling-class ideology intent on reducing men and women to political quiescence. His own episodic, open-ended theatrical forms are designed to challenge this fatalism.[72]

In an essay entitled 'Nature, Humanism and Tragedy', Alain Robbe-Grillet complains that Albert Camus's notion of tragic absurdity serves as a devious device for recuperating non-meaning for meaning. Tragedy, he claims, is a last-ditch attempt to see the distance between Nature and humanity in moral terms, treating it as a matter of angst and estrangement rather than simply as a fact.[73] Yet distance is not disseverance. The plain truth, Robbe-Grillet insists, is that there is nothing lacking or defective about this condition – no painful fissure, ontological void or ominously absent deity. When it comes to the death of God, tragedy perceives the problem not as his non-existence but as his cryptic refusal to respond to his creatures. Simple absence is charged with bogus depth. In similar vein, Roland Barthes accuses tragic art of being 'merely a means of "recovering" human misery, of subsuming and therefore justifying it in the form of a necessity, a wisdom or a purification . . . nothing is more insidious than tragedy'.[74] There are, in fact, a good many things in the world more insidious than *The Changeling* or *Titus Andronicus*, but Barthes's caustic comment is nonetheless refreshing. No one familiar with the relentless idealising of the tragic in the culture of modern Europe could fail to appreciate its candour.

Theodor Adorno comments that 'a successful [art]work . . . is not one which resolves objective contradictions in a spurious harmony, but one which expresses the idea of harmony negatively by embodying the contradictions, pure and uncompromised, in its innermost structure'.[75] In similar vein, John Haffenden points out that the William Empson of *Seven Types of Ambiguity* 'is not looking to *settle* ambiguities, as if they represent some kind of literary indigestion, but to celebrate the polysemy of poetry, its weft and warp of mixed meanings'.[76] Jacques Lacan dismisses the Hegelian notion of tragic reconciliation, observing that the topic of tragedy is where Hegel is at his least impressive.[77] Slavoj Žižek, Lacan's emissary on earth, is equally scornful of such syntheses. In his view, tragedy stages the violent clash of mutually incommensurable positions, and as such is a stranger to rational negotiation or ethical consensus.[78] The Irish philosopher William Desmond finds in tragedy 'one of the ultimate forms of being at a loss' and sees tragic knowledge as 'shattering every naive faith in the basic intelligibility, indeed value of being'. It is a form of consciousness which 'brings home the permeability of all things by loss',[79] and as such eludes the grasp of philosophy. Nietzsche, as we have seen, is another thinker for whom the tragic outflanks the philosophical; but this is because it speaks to his mind of deeper matters, whereas for Desmond it is the trauma of the tragic which strikes such reflections mute.

There are, as it happens, strikingly few instances of tragic drama which conform to the model proposed by Schiller, Schelling, Hölderlin and their colleagues. Joshua Billings points out that no art-form has been more intensively theorised than tragedy, but neither, one might add, is there one which betrays such flagrant discrepancies between theory and practice.[80] Raymond Williams writes that 'the most remarkable fact about the post-feudal idea of tragedy is its distance from the major creative developments in actual tragic writing'.[81] Not many tragic protagonists, from Prometheus to Captain Ahab, resign themselves with heroic fortitude to their fate, seeing in it the secret working of a benign Absolute. If this were definitive of the form, Plato would not have needed to propose the censoring of whole swathes of such poetry as morally and politically subversive, a source of dissent, irreverence, pessimism, emotional self-indulgence, unstable identity, unbridled passion and a danger to the rational harmony of the soul. Indeed, the state of mind of the Schillerian or Schellingian tragic hero, possessed of an equipoise of soul that no external power can endanger, is not far from the Platonic ideal of the good life.

In a valuable study entitled *Tragedy and Theory*, Michelle Gellrich shows how the theory of tragic drama over the centuries has sought to sanitise the practice of it, neutralising its moral outrage, stifling its conflicts, defusing its disruptiveness with anodyne appeals to virtue, rationality and social harmony and tidying up a whole series of aporias and ambiguities in the texts themselves.[82] The philosophy of tragedy, one might suggest, has played Apollo to the Dionysus of the practice. Aristotle, Gellrich points out, has little to say of the form's agonistic features. If tragedy is not disinfected in this way, she argues, it risks being morally unedifying. Many an early-modern observer regards the form as morally and socially degenerate, a dispiriting narrative of chaos, insurgency and political volatility. Hegel, Gellrich notes, is the first prominent theorist of tragedy to attend to its conflicts and contradictions – though he does so with an eye to a final *détente*.

Tragedy has been seen as an expression of nausea at human existence, or as a tranquil transcendence of it. There are those for whom it involves a glorification of death and self-sacrifice, a disdain for human mortality or a glad-hearted submission to authority. One can find in it an apologia for unhappiness, a salutary fostering of illusion or a plea for the paltriness of reason. It may take the form of a malicious delight at seeing men and women hacked to death, or be dismissed as a scene of squalid farce. It has been praised as an epiphany of infinite freedom, a victory over Nature or a clear-eyed embracing of the inevitable. Whatever version one chooses, it does not sound on the face of it the most humane, enlightened of art-forms. It is fortunate, then, that most tragic art fails to conform to these doctrines, and that not all critics subscribe to them in any case. Writing in the early-modern period, the Earl of Shaftesbury, a progressive Whig deeply hostile to Tory corruption at court, regards tragedy as a vehicle for republican sentiments, warning as it does against despotism and venality in high places. It is a corrective to a Tory grovelling at the feet of power. Shaftesbury thus joins an honourable tradition, one particularly marked in the medieval period, for which tragedy warns the populace against the vices and unbridled passions of the mighty.[83]

One does not need to appeal to the progressively minded, however, to recognise just how gentrified a view of tragedy is taken by the tradition which flows from Schiller to the early Lukács. The most harrowing forms of tragic art deal in distress for which no solace is possible, injuries which the passage of time will not erase, relationships which are irretrievably broken, states of desolation which refuse all comfort. It is perverse to withhold the title of tragedy from such art simply because it refuses reconciliation. On the contrary, it is part of its integrity that it does so. Rowan Williams speaks in *The Tragic Imagination* of tragedy as 'mak[ing] sense of pain'.[84] It is a ceremony by which we seek to share, honour, memorialise and find some meaning in mortal harm, but Williams is equally conscious of what is inaccessible about that harm even to the most empathetic of onlookers. Tragic art requires us to feel the misfortune of others, but it also demands a respect for the opaqueness of their sorrow.

Indeed, one might argue that some forms of suffering, not least acute physical pain, are manifestations of meaninglessness, and in this sense part of what is traditionally meant by the demonic. They represent local unravellings of the cosmos, signs of a crazed desire to return the whole of Creation back to chaos. Rowan Williams, paraphrasing the theologian Donald MacKinnon, writes of 'senseless, inexplicable, unjustifiable, unassimilable pain, pain which is, so to speak, non-negotiable'.[85] As with Iago confronting Othello, the demonic is affronted by the very existence of meaning and value, which it finds fraudulent as well as repellent. Virtue strikes it as ludicrously pretentious. It is just a lot of high-minded cant thinly concealing the gross operations of appetite. The demonic, in a word, is a form of nihilism or cynicism – one which revels in absurdity, wallows in the farcical, sniggers at love and pity and cannot be redeemed because it fails to grasp the meaning of redemption.

A surreally brief history of the notion of conflict might begin with the pre-Socratics, for whom the universe consists of strife without synthesis. Antithetical forces exist in equilibrium. From classical antiquity to the age of Enlightenment, unity and symmetry are highly prized, while dissonance and disruption pose a threat to stability. For the Idealists, Romantics and nineteenth-century teleologists, by contrast, struggle and waste have their part to play in the felicitous evolution of human history. Unity remains the keynote, but one which can finally incorporate divisions. In late modernity, as we have seen, this faith in reconciliation is increasingly censured as fantasy or false utopia.

What follows is the culture of postmodernism, for which conflict and contradiction are no longer pressing questions. The emphasis falls instead on difference and diversity. The postmodern disposition, unlike its modernist predecessor, is not for the most part a tragic one. Its aversion to 'deep' subjectivity does not sit easily with spiritual torment or ontological angst. If it does not believe in redemption, it is because it can see nothing to be redeemed. Such high-toned metaphysical talk rings hollow in a world of social media and high finance. Besides, the relativist spirit of postmodernism is uneasy with the absolutism of death and the irreparable nature of tragic loss. The nobility of the tragic grates on postmodernism's populist sensibility, while its exalted rhetoric offends post-modernism's low-key, laid-back mood. There are no death-dealing clashes of vision or conviction, since postmodern culture suspects that vision is idly utopian and all conviction incipiently dogmatic. Since it distrusts the idea of unity as falsely essentialist, the prospect of resolving hostilities has no great appeal. For much the same reason, it is also largely indif-ferent to the concept of political solidarity. If postmodernism is rightly cautious of the more triumphalist aspects of the tragic, it is largely for the wrong reasons.

Sounder reasons for such scepticism are surely not hard to come by. The legacy which passes from Kant to Heidegger is among the most fruitful, ambitious currents of thought in modern intellectual history. Its reflections on tragedy, however, fail to reveal it at its most persuasive. For the most part, philos-ophers of tragedy have hacked down the range and diversity of the art to suit their own ethico-political ends. What then emerges is a version of the tragic which serves largely to suppress tragedy in the commonplace sense of the word. Comedy in art is not far removed from comedy in life, but in the case of tragedy, as we have seen already, there is a gulf between its aesthetic and everyday senses. Not only that, but the everyday use of the word yields a more faithful account of most tragic drama than do most of the theories we have examined. Common opinion, for example, is surely right to hold that the irreparable is more tragic than the resolvable, which is not to suggest that the latter has no place. This ideology of the tragic does a disservice to those whose plight proves to be beyond repair – to all those caught up in conflicts which turn out to be irreducible to a unity of opposites. It fails to grant the inconsolable the respect they deserve.

NOTES

1 DID TRAGEDY DIE?

1. See Terry Eagleton, *Sweet Violence: The Idea of the Tragic* (Oxford, 2003), p. 71.
2. Blair Hoxby, *What Was Tragedy?* (Oxford, 2015), p. 7.
3. Though Edith Hall argues that Aristotle's *Poetics*, which does not situate tragedy in its public context, is already beginning to universalise the form. See Edith Hall, 'Is There a *Polis* in Aristotle's *Poetics?*', in M.S. Silk (ed.), *Tragedy and the Tragic* (Oxford, 1991).
4. See Barbara Cassin, 'Greeks and Romans: Paradigms of the Past in Arendt and Heidegger', *Comparative Civilisations Review* no. 22 (1990), p. 49.
5. Hannah Arendt, *The Human Condition* (Chicago, 1958), p. 188.
6. For an informative survey of ancient tragedy, see Emily Wilson (ed.), *A Cultural History of Tragedy*, vol. 1: *In Antiquity* (London, 2019).
7. Jean-Pierre Vernant and Pierre Vidal-Naquet, *Myth and Tragedy in Ancient Greece* (New York, 1960), p. 185. For tragedy as a political institution, see also J. Peter Euben, 'Introduction', in J. Peter Euben (ed.), *Greek Tragedy and Political Theory* (Berkeley, 1986).
8. Rainer Friedrich, 'Everything to Do with Dionysus', in Silk (ed.), *Tragedy and the Tragic*, p. 263. See also Simon Goldhill, 'The Great Dionysus and Civic Ideology', in John J. Winkler and Froma I. Zeitlin

(eds), *Nothing to Do with Dionysus? Athenian Drama in its Social Context* (Princeton, NJ, 1990).

9. See Hannah Arendt, *Between Past and Future* (New York, 1978), p. 154. See also Robert C. Pirro, *Hannah Arendt and the Politics of Tragedy* (DeKalb, IL, 2001), esp. ch. 2.

10. For Lessing's ideas on theatre, see G.E. Lessing, *The Hamburg Dramaturgy* (New York, 1962).

11. See Philippe Lacoue-Labarthe, 'On the Sublime', *Postmodernism: ICA Documents 4* (London, 1986), p. 9.

12. On modern substitutes for religion, see Terry Eagleton, *Culture and the Death of God* (New Haven, CT and London, 2014).

13. Arthur Schopenhauer, *The World as Will and Representation* (New York, 1969), vol. 1, pp. 254–5 and vol. 2, p. 437.

14. Quoted by George J. Becker (ed.), *Documents of Modern Literary Realism* (Princeton, NJ, 1973), p. 118. For a study of social class in tragedy, see Edith Hall, 'To Fall from High to Low Estate? Tragedy and Social Class in Historical Perspective', *PMLA* vol. 129, no. 4 (October 2014).

15. See Lessing, *The Hamburg Dramaturgy*, pp. 178–94.

16. For some exemplary works of this kind, see A.C. Bradley, *Shakespearean Tragedy* (London, 1904); D.D. Raphael, *The Paradox of Tragedy* (London, 1960); Dorothea Krook, *Elements of Tragedy* (New Haven, CT and London, 1969); F.L. Lucas, *Tragedy: Serious Drama in Relation to Aristotle's 'Poetics'* (London, 1966); Walter Kerr, *Tragedy and Comedy* (New York, 1968); and Joseph Wood Krutch, *The Modern Temper* (London, 1930).

17. George Steiner, *The Death of Tragedy* (London, 1961), p. 130.

18. See Edmund Burke, *A Philosophical Enquiry into the Origin of our Ideas of the Sublime and Beautiful* (London, 1958), p. 46.

19. Bertolt Brecht, *The Messingkauf Dialogues* (London, 1965), p. 47.

20. See Glenn W. Most, 'Generating Genres: The Idea of the Tragic', in Mary Depew and Dirk Oblink (eds), *Matrices of Genre: Authors, Canons, and Society* (Cambridge, MA and London, 2000).

21. For the difference between the two, see Terry Eagleton, *Hope without Optimism* (London and New Haven, CT, 2015), especially ch. 1.

22. Christopher Norris, *William Empson and the Philosophy of Literary Criticism* (London, 1978), p. 91. The comment is intended to endorse such rationalism rather than to criticise it.

23. Steiner, *The Death of Tragedy*, p. 243.
24. See Roger Scruton, *The Uses of Pessimism and the Danger of False Hope* (London, 2010).
25. Steiner, *The Death of Tragedy*, p. 128.
26. William Empson, *Some Versions of Pastoral* (London, 1935), p. 12.
27. See Sigmund Freud, *The Interpretation of Dreams*, in James Strachey (ed.), *The Standard Edition of the Complete Psychological Works of Sigmund Freud* (London, 1953–74), vol. 4, p. 262.
28. Richard Halpern, *Eclipse of Action: Tragedy and Political Economy* (Chicago and London, 2017), p. 2.
29. See George Steiner, ' "Tragedy", Reconsidered', in Rita Felski (ed.), *Rethinking Tragedy* (Baltimore, MD, 2008), p. 37.
30. See Susan Sontag, 'The Death of Tragedy', in Sontag, *Against Interpretation* (London, 1994).
31. See Albert Camus, 'On the Future of Tragedy', in Camus, *Lyrical and Critical Essays* (New York, 1968).
32. Agnes Heller and Ferenc Feher, *The Grandeur and Twilight of Radical Universalism* (London, 1991), p. 311.
33. For a useful survey of the subject see Thomas Van Laan, 'The Death of Tragedy Myth', *Journal of Dramatic Theory and Criticism* (spring, 1991).
34. Steiner, *The Death of Tragedy*, p. 129.
35. Kathleen M. Sands, 'Tragedy, Theology, and Feminism', in Felski (ed.), *Rethinking Tragedy*, p. 89.
36. Miriam Leonard, *Tragic Modernities* (Cambridge, MA and London, 2015), p. 10.
37. Gilles Deleuze, *Nietzsche and Philosophy* (London, 1983), p. 18.
38. See Raymond Williams, *Modern Tragedy* (London, 1966), pp. 61–7.
39. Steiner, *The Death of Tragedy*, p. 10.
40. Steiner, ' "Tragedy", Reconsidered', p. 40.
41. Perhaps I should add for the sake of intellectual justice that Steiner is one of the commentators on tragedy I enjoy reading most – not, as should be clear, because I agree with much of what he claims, but for his magnificently burnished prose style, full of brio, bravura, commanding rhetoric, lapidary turns of phrase and brilliantly inventive verbal touches. He is one of the last in a tradition of the critic as creative writer.
42. Williams, *Modern Tragedy*, pp. 45–6.

43. See Friedrich Hölderlin, *Essays and Letters* (London, 2009), p. 146.

44. Karl Marx, *The Eighteenth Brumaire of Louis Bonaparte* (London, 1984), p. 11.

45. Vernant and Vidal-Naquet, *Myth and Tragedy in Ancient Greece*, p. 33.

46. See Bernard Williams, *Shame and Necessity* (Berkeley, CA, 1993), pp. 16–17.

47. Simon Goldhill, 'The Ends of Tragedy', in Joshua Billings and Miriam Leonard (eds), *Tragedy and the Idea of Modernity* (Oxford, 2015), p. 233.

48. Raymond Williams, *Politics and Letters* (London, 1979), p. 212.

49. See Søren Kierkegaard, *Either/Or* (Princeton, NJ, 1959), esp. pp. 140–9.

50. Felski (ed.), *Rethinking Tragedy*, p. 9.

51. See Arthur Miller, 'Tragedy and the Common Man', in *The Theater Essays of Arthur Miller* (New York, 1978), p. 215.

52. Quoted by Raymond Williams, *Modern Tragedy*, p. 116.

53. Quoted by Anne Paolucci and Henry Paolucci (eds), *Hegel on Tragedy* (New York, 1962), p. 50.

54. H.H. Gerth and C. Wright Mills (eds), *Max Weber: Essays in Sociology* (London, 1970), p. 149.

55. See Slavoj Žižek, *The Fragile Absolute* (London, 2008), p. 40.

56. Quoted by Raymond Williams, *Modern Tragedy*, p. 116.

57. As the nineteenth-century Russian critic N.G. Chernishevsky comments, 'The tragic has nothing essentially in common with the idea of fate or necessity. In real life, tragedy is most commonly accidental, [and] does not follow as a necessary consequence of preceding events'; quoted in Becker (ed.), *Documents of Modern Literary Realism*, p. 78. It is a rare observation among commentators on tragedy.

58. For the everyday use of the word 'tragedy', see Robert C. Pirro, *The Politics of Tragedy and Democratic Citizenship* (London, 2011), pp. 12–14.

59. Since I shall be using the Lacanian triad of Imaginary, Symbolic and Real in this study, an explanatory note on these concepts is perhaps in order. By the Imaginary, Lacan means our commonplace relations to objects, including other persons, which involve such features as reflection, resemblance, rivalry, correspondence, identification and the like, and which contain an inescapable degree of illusion and misrepresentation. The Symbolic (or symbolic order) is the realm of language,

kinship, social roles and regulations by which we are allotted an identity, while the Real, which is strictly speaking unrepresentable, signifies the trauma of severance from the mother and submission to the
Law of the Father, by which we achieve individual selfhood – a
primordial wounding which generates the process of lack and loss
which we call desire, and which can also be seen as the opening up of
the unconscious and the unleashing of the death drive.

60. For an account of Lacan's reading of Antigone, see David Farrell Krell,
    The Tragic Absolute (Bloomington, IN, 2005), ch. 11.

61. Slavoj Žižek, *Did Somebody Say Totalitarianism?* (London and New
    York, 2001), p. 157. For a critique of Žižek's approach to Antigone, see
    Yannis Stavrakakis, *The Lacanian Left* (Edinburgh, 2007), pp. 114–34.
    For an illuminating set of essays on *Antigone*, see S.E. Wilmer and
    Audrone Zukauskaite (eds), *Interrogating Antigone in Postmodern
    Philosophy and Criticism* (Oxford, 2010).

62. Žižek, *Did Somebody Say Totalitarianism?*, p. 158.

63. See Slavoj Žižek, *The Parallax View* (Cambridge, MA, 2006), pp. 104–5.

64. See Charles Taylor, *The Sources of the Self* (Cambridge, 1989), p. 213.

65. Žižek, *The Parallax View*, p. 400.

66. Žižek argues such a case in an essay entitled 'A Plea for Ethical
    Violence' in the online journal *The Bible and Critical Theory*, vol. 1,
    no. 1 (Monash University Epress).

67. See Rolf Tiedemann and Hermann Schweppenhauser (eds), *Walter
    Benjamin: Gesammelte Schriften* (Frankfurt am Main, 1966), vol. 1,
    p. 583.

2 INCEST AND ARITHMETIC

1. The issue is examined with exemplary thoroughness in Charles Segal,
   Tragedy and Civilisation (Cambridge, MA and London, 1981), ch. 7.
   For an illuminating philosophical discussion of riddles in general, see
   Stephen Mulhall, *The Great Riddle: Wittgenstein and Nonsense, Theology
   and Philosophy* (Oxford, 2015), Lecture Two.

2. Though some scholars hold that there is no puzzle here – that the
   surviving eye-witness lied when he saw that the solitary killer had
   become king.

3. Maurice Merleau-Ponty, *Humanism and Terror* (Boston, MA, 1969),
   p. 183.

4. See Jean-Pierre Vernant, 'Ambiguity and Reversal: On the Enigmatic Structure of Oedipus Rex', in E. Segal (ed.), *Oxford Readings in Greek Tragedy* (Oxford, 1983).

5. Froma Zeitlin, 'Thebes: Theater of Self and Society in Athenian Drama', in Euben (ed.), *Greek Tragedy and Political Theory*, p. 111.

6. It is remarkable how often the subject of incest crops up in tragedy – no doubt among other reasons because of its sheer sensationalism. A far from exhaustive inventory of examples would include Euripides' *Hippolytus*, Shakespeare's *Richard III*, *Hamlet*, *Cymbeline* and *Pericles*, Lope de Vega's *Punishment without Revenge*, John Ford's *'Tis Pity She's a Whore*, Thomas Middleton's *Women Beware Women* and *The Revenger's Tragedy*, Cyril Tourneur's *The Atheist's Tragedy*, Thomas Otway's *The Orphans*, John Dryden's *Aureng-Zebe*, Jean Racine's *Phèdre*, Vittorio Alfieri's *Mirra*, Schiller's *Don Carlos*, Shelley's *The Cenci*, Byron's *Cain*, Ibsen's *Ghosts*, Eugene O'Neill's *Desire Under the Elms* and *Mourning Becomes Electra*, and Arthur Miller's *A View from the Bridge*. There are also hints of incest, or near-misses, in Ford's *The Broken Heart*, John Webster's *The Duchess of Malfi* and Gotthold Lessing's *Nathan the Wise*. Richard McCabe notes what he calls the 'astonishing prevalence' of the incest theme in his *Incest, Drama, and Nature's Law* (Oxford, 1993), p. 4.

7. McCabe, *Incest, Drama, and Nature's Law*, p. 70.

8. Roland Barthes, *Sade, Fourier, Loyola* (London, 1977), p. 137.

9. Franco Moretti, *Signs Taken as Wonders* (London, 1983), p. 74.

10. Eric L. Santner, *The Weight of All Flesh* (Oxford, 2016), p. 49.

11. Quoted by Iain Topliss, 'Oedipus/Freud and the Psychoanalytic Narrative', in T. Collits (ed.), *Agamemnon's Mask: Greek Tragedy and Beyond* (New Delhi, 2007), p. 103.

12. Quoted by Geoffrey Green, *Literary Criticism and the Structure of History* (Lincoln, NE and London, 1982), p. 79.

3 TRAGIC TRANSITIONS

1. See Raymond Williams, *Marxism and Literature* (Oxford, 1977), pp. 121–7.

2. Albert Camus, *Selected Essays and Notebooks* (Harmondsworth, 1970), p. 199.

3. Claudio Magris, 'A Cryptogram of its Age', *New Left Review* no. 95 (September/October, 2015), p. 96.

4. See Pirro, *Hannah Arendt and the Politics of Tragedy*, pp. 176–7, and M.I. Finley, *Politics in the Ancient World* (Cambridge, 1983).
5. See Charles Segal, *Oedipus Tyrannus: Tragic Heroism and the Limits of Knowledge* (New York and Oxford, 2001). Classical scholars are divided, however, on the question of how much of a rationalist Sophocles is. See Peter J. Ahronsdorf, *Greek Tragedy and Political Philosophy* (Cambridge, 2009), ch. 1. See also Christopher Rocco, *Tragedy and Enlightenment* (Berkeley, CA, 1997) and Bernard A. Knox, *Oedipus at Thebes* (New Haven, CT and London, 1998)
6. Hoxby, *What Was Tragedy?*, p. 38.
7. Vernant and Vidal-Naquet, *Myth and Tragedy in Ancient Greece*, p. 184.
8. Simon Goldhill, 'Generalising about Tragedy', in Felski (ed.), *Rethinking Tragedy*, p. 59.
9. Ibid., p. 54.
10. Joshua Billings, *Genealogy of the Tragic* (Princeton, NJ and Oxford, 2014), p. 181.
11. Vernant and Vidal-Naquet, *Myth and Tragedy in Ancient Greece*, p. 117.
12. Ibid., p. 139.
13. See Jean-Joseph Goux, *Oedipus, Philosopher* (Stanford, CA, 1993), ch. 1.
14. Williams, *Shame and Necessity*, p. 164.
15. For Gramsci's variable uses of the concept of hegemony, see Perry Anderson, 'The Antinomies of Antonio Gramsci', *New Left Review* no. 100 (November 1976/January 1977).
16. E.M.W. Tillyard, *The Elizabethan World Picture* (London, 1943), p. 5.
17. Moretti, *Signs Taken as Wonders*, p. 28.
18. See J.G. Herder, *Selected Writings on Aesthetics* (Princeton, NJ, 2009), pp. 298–9.
19. Moretti, *Signs Taken as Wonders*, p. 69.
20. Raymond Williams, *The Long Revolution* (London, 1961), p. 252.
21. Bart van Es, 'Too Much Changed', *Times Literary Supplement* (2 September 2016), p. 14. For a suggestive account of Shakespeare and historical transition, see Paul Mason, *PostCapitalism: A Guide to Our Future* (London, 2015), pp. 235–6.
22. Carl Schmitt, *Hamlet or Hecuba?* (New York, 2009), p. 52.
23. I have developed these ideas more fully in my *William Shakespeare* (Oxford, 1986).
24. For a valuable study of the revenge tragedy of the period, see John Kerrigan, *Revenge Tragedy: Aeschylus to Armageddon* (Oxford, 1996).

25. See Lucien Goldmann, *Racine* (Cambridge, 1972), p. 10. For a useful commentary on Goldmann see Mitchell Cohen, *The Wager of Lucien Goldmann: Tragedy, Dialectics, and a Hidden God* (Princeton, NJ, 1994).

26. Simon Critchley, 'Phaedra's Malaise', in Felski (ed.), *Rethinking Tragedy*, p. 193.

27. Steiner, *The Death of Tragedy*, p. 80.

28. See Stephen Halliday, 'Plato's Repudiation of the Tragic', in Silk (ed.), *Tragedy and the Tragic*.

29. Friedrich, 'Everything to Do with Dionysus', p. 277.

30. Billings, *Genealogy of the Tragic*, p. 177.

31. See Karl Marx and Friedrich Engels, *On Literature and Art* (Moscow, 1976), pp. 98–101. See also S.S. Prawer, *Karl Marx and World Literature* (Oxford, 1976), ch. 9.

32. 'Fate and Character', in Walter Benjamin, *One-Way Street and Other Writings* (London, 1978), p. 127.

33. See Walter Benjamin, 'Trauerspiel and Tragedy', in Walter Benjamin, *Selected Writings*, vol. 1: *1913–1926* (Cambridge, MA and London, 1996).

34. Timothy J. Reiss, *Tragedy and Truth* (New Haven, CT and London, 1980), p. 284.

35. Ibid., p. 302.

36. See Fredric Jameson, *A Singular Modernity* (London and New York, 2012), Part 1, and Perry Anderson, 'Modernity and Revolution', *New Left Review* no. 144 (March–April, 1984).

37. For my purposes here, I treat Ibsenite naturalism *à la* Georg Lukács as a form of modernism.

38. See Franco Moretti, *The Bourgeois* (London and New York, 2013), p. 171.

39. Benjamin Constant, 'Reflections on Tragedy', in Barry V. Daniels (ed.), *Revolution in the Theatre* (Westport, CT, 1983), p. 107.

40. Raymond Williams, *Modern Tragedy*, p. 87.

41. Werner Sombart, *The Quintessence of Capitalism* (London, 1915), pp. 202 and 22.

42. See Moretti, *The Bourgeois*, p. 170.

43. See Jennifer Wallace, *The Cambridge Introduction to Tragedy* (Cambridge, 2007), p. 75.

44. Camus, 'On the Future of Tragedy', p. 298.

4 FRUITFUL FALSEHOODS

1. David Hume, *Treatise of Human Nature* (Oxford, 1960), p. 566.
2. Edmund Burke, 'Letter to Sir Hercules Langrishe', in R.B. McDowell (ed.), *The Writings and Speeches of Edmund Burke*, vol. 9 (Oxford, 1991), p. 614.
3. Edmund Burke, *Reflections on the Revolution in France*, in Francis Canavan (ed.), *Select Works of Edmund Burke* (Indianapolis, IN, 1999), vol. 2, p. 170.
4. Matthew Arnold, 'The Incompatibles', in R.H. Super (ed.), *The Complete Prose Works of Matthew Arnold*, vol. 9: *English Literature and Irish Politics* (Ann Arbor, MI, 1973), p. 243.
5. Blaise Pascal, *Pensées* (Harmondsworth, 1966), pp. 46–7.
6. See Hans Reiss (ed.), *Kant's Political Writings* (Cambridge, 1970), p. 143.
7. Quoted by Keith Ansell Pearson, *Nietzsche* (London, 2005), p. 55.
8. I have discussed this question in more detail in Eagleton, *Culture and the Death of God*, ch. 1.
9. See David Hume, *Dialogues Concerning Natural Religion and the Natural History of Religion* (Oxford, 1993), p. 153.
10. Max Weber, 'Science as a Vocation', in Gerth and Wright Mills (eds), *Max Weber*, p. 155.
11. Duc de la Rochefoucauld, *Maxims and Moral Reflections* (London, 1749), p. 36.
12. Spinoza, *Ethics* (London, 2000), p. 62.
13. Antoine-Nicolas de Condorcet, *Sketch for a Historical Picture of the Progress of the Human Mind* (London, 1955), p. 109.
14. See Althusser's remarks on ideology in *For Marx* (London, 1969), p. 234, and the essay 'Ideology and Ideological State Apparatuses' in *Lenin and Philosophy* (London, 1971).
15. *The Wit and Wisdom of Oscar Wilde* (London, 1960), p. 52.
16. Ibid., p. 56.
17. Roger Scruton, *Spinoza* (Oxford, 2002), p. 76.
18. J.M. Synge, *The Playboy of the Western World and Other Plays* (Oxford, 1995), p. 60.
19. See G.W.F. Hegel, *Phenomenology of Spirit* (Oxford, 1977), pp. 22–3.
20. John Roberts, *The Necessity of Errors* (London, 2011), p. 204.
21. Iris Murdoch, *The Sovereignty of the Good* (London, 2006), p. 91.
22. See Žižek, *The Fragile Absolute*, ch. 8.

23. Quentin Skinner, *Machiavelli: A Very Short Introduction* (Oxford, 2000), p. 47.
24. Friedrich Nietzsche, *The Joyful Wisdom* (London, 1910), p. 279.
25. Friedrich Nietzsche, *The Genealogy of Morals*, in Walter Kaufmann (ed.), *Basic Writings of Nietzsche* (New York, 1968), p. 573.
26. John Gray, *Straw Dogs* (London, 2003), p. 27.
27. See, for example, William James, 'Pragmatism's Conception of Truth', in *William James: Pragmatism and Other Writings* (London, 2000).
28. Friedrich Nietzsche, *The Birth of Tragedy*, in Kaufmann (ed.), *Basic Writings of Nietzsche*, p. 60.
29. Friedrich Nietzsche, *The Will to Power* (New York, 1968), p. 435.
30. Deleuze, *Nietzsche and Philosophy*, pp. 102–3.
31. Quoted by Simon Critchley and Jamieson Webster, *The Hamlet Doctrine* (London, 2013), p. 16.
32. See Hans Vaihinger, *The Philosophy of 'As If'* (London, 1924).
33. Georges Sorel, *Reflections on Violence* (New York, 1947), p. 35.
34. Ibid., p. 133.
35. I.A. Richards, *Mencius on the Mind* (London and New York, 2001), p. 66.
36. I.A. Richards, *Coleridge on Imagination* (London and New York, 2001), p. 134.
37. William Empson, *Argufying: Essays on Literature and Culture* (Iowa City, 1987), p. 198.
38. Wallace Stevens, *Opus Posthumous* (New York, 1957), p. 163.
39. See Martin Heidegger, 'The Origin of the Work of Art', in David Farrell Krell (ed.), *Martin Heidegger: Basic Writings* (New York, 1977).
40. Though one on which I naively heaped unqualified praise in my first book. See Terence (sic) Eagleton, *The New Left Church* (London, 1966), ch. 1
41. See Žižek, *The Fragile Absolute*, p. 40.
42. F.R. Leavis, *The Common Pursuit* (London, 2008), p. 152.
43. I.A. Richards, *Principles of Literary Criticism* (London and New York, 2001), p. 217.
44. See Žižek, *The Fragile Absolute*, p. 39.
45. Arthur Miller, *Plays 1* (London, 2014), p. 33.

5 THE INCONSOLABLE

1. John Stuart Mill, *On Liberty and Other Essays* (Oxford, 1991), p. 54.

2. Helen Gardner, *Religion and Literature* (London, 1971), p. 24.
3. Miguel de Beistegui and Simon Sparks (eds), *Philosophy and Tragedy* (London and New York, 2000), p. 11.
4. Richards, *Principles of Literary Criticism*, pp. 217–18
5. Walter Kaufmann, *Tragedy and Philosophy* (New York, 1968), p. 182.
6. Ludwig Wittgenstein, *Culture and Value* (Oxford, 1998), p. 12e.
7. See Steiner, *The Death of Tragedy*, p. 122. There are, to be sure, a number of well-known exceptions to this stricture.
8. Goldhill, 'The Ends of Tragedy', p. 233. There is also an illuminating account of the subject in Miriam Leonard, *Tragic Modernities* (Cambridge, Mass. and London, 2015), Ch. 3.
9. John Macmurray, *The Self as Agent* (London, 1969), p. 55.
10. F.W.J. Schelling, *System of Transcendental Idealism* (Charlottesville, VA, 1978), p. 35.
11. Dennis Schmidt, *On Germans and Other Greeks* (Bloomington, IN, 2001), p. 15.
12. See Max Scheler, 'On the Tragic', in R.W. Corrigan (ed.), *Tragedy: Vision and Form* (New York, 1965).
13. Friedrich Schlegel, *'Lucinda' and the Fragments* (Minneapolis, MN, 1971), p. 150.
14. Ludwig Wittgenstein, 'Lecture on Ethics', *Philosophical Review* no. 74 (1965), p. 8.
15. See Friedrich Schiller, *'Naive and Sentimental Poetry' and 'On the Sublime': Two Essays* (New York, 1967). For a valuable account of the German nineteenth-century tradition of tragic thought, see Vassilis Lambropoulos, *The Tragic Idea* (London, 2006). See also Julian Young, *The Philosophy of Tragedy from Plato to Žižek* (Cambridge, 2013). There is also an illuminating account of the subject in Leonard, *Tragic Modernities*, ch. 2.
16. See David Roberts, *Art and Enlightenment* (Lincoln, NE and London, 1991), pp. 9–10.
17. Simon Critchley, 'The Tragedy of Misrecognition', in Billings and Leonard (eds), *Tragedy and the Idea of Modernity*, p. 253.
18. See Allan Megill, *Prophets of Extremity* (Berkeley, CA, 1985), p. 58.
19. A useful translation of some of Schiller's essays on aesthetics is to be found in Walter Hinderer and Daniel O. Dahlstrom (eds), *Friedrich Schiller: Essays* (New York, 1993).
20. For Schelling's aesthetic thought, see the Tenth Letter of his *Letters on Dogmatism and Criticism*, reproduced in Schmidt, *On Germans and*

Other Greeks, and Friedrich Schelling, *Philosophy of Art* (Minneapolis, MN, 1989). Suggestive studies of Schelling's thought are Leonardo V. Distaso, *The Paradox of Existence: Philosophy and Aesthetics in the Young Schelling* (Dordrecht, 2004), and Devin Zane Shaw, *Freedom and Nature in Schelling's Philosophy of Art* (London, 2010).

21. Schelling, *Philosophy of Art*, p. 251.
22. See ibid., p. 249.
23. The essay can be found in Camus, *Lyrical and Critical Essays*.
24. Some of Hölderlin's writings on aesthetic matters can be found in T. Pfau (ed.), *Friedrich Hölderlin: Essays and Letters on Theory* (Albany, NY, 1988). See also his early novel *Hyperion, or the Hermit in Greece* (New York, 1965).
25. Quoted by Schmidt, *On Germans and Other Greeks*, p. 133.
26. See Hölderlin's essay 'The Significance of Tragedy', in Pfau (ed.) *Hölderlin: Essays and Letters*.
27. See Friedrich Theodor Vischer, *Aesthetik, oder, Wissenschaften des Schonen* (Stuttgart, 1858), pp. 277–333.
28. See K.W.F. Solger, *Vorlesungen uber Aesthetik* (Leipzig, 1829), pp. 296–7.
29. Quoted by Billings, *Genealogy of the Tragic*, p. 189.
30. See Paul, Second Letter to the Corinthians, 4: 7.
31. Even Seneca's work, however, has been enlisted as therapeutic, persuading the audience to confront their demons and purging their passions. See G. Staley, *Seneca and the Idea of Tragedy* (Oxford, 2010).
32. Paolucci and Paolucci (eds), *Hegel on Tragedy*, p. 51.
33. Quoted by Billlings, *Genealogy of the Tragic*, p. 150. For a useful account of Hegel on tragedy, see Stephen Houlgate, 'Hegel's Theory of Tragedy', in Stephen Houlgate (ed.), *Hegel and the Arts* (Evanston, IL, 2007). Rowan Williams makes out a case critical of the reconciliatory view of Hegel's tragic aesthetics in his *The Tragic Imagination* (Oxford, 2016), ch. 3.
34. Beistegui and Sparks (eds), *Philosophy and Tragedy*, p. 33.
35. See Peter Szondi, *An Essay on the Tragic* (Stanford, CA, 2002), p. 20. See also G.W.F. Hegel, *Aesthetics: Lectures on Fine Art*, 2 vols (Oxford, 1975).
36. Quoted by Szondi, *An Essay on the Tragic*, p. 27.
37. Schmidt, *On Germans and Other Greeks*, p. 90.
38. See Roberts, *The Necessity of Errors*, pp. 203–4.
39. See Vischer, *Aesthetik*, pp. 277–333.

40. See Friedrich Hebbel, *Mein Wort Uber das Drama* (Hamburg, 1843), pp. 34–5. An essay remains to be written on why so many German Idealist thinkers are called Friedrich.

41. Quoted in Paolucci and Paolucci (eds), *Hegel on Tragedy*, p. 51.

42. For an inquiry into the idea of irresolvable dilemmas, see Rosalind Hursthouse, *On Virtue Ethics* (Oxford, 1999), ch. 3.

43. Quoted by Raymond Williams, *Modern Tragedy*, p. 38.

44. Quoted in Paolucci and Paolucci (eds), *Hegel on Tragedy*, p. 50.

45. See A. Maria van Erp Taalman Kip, 'The Unity of the *Oresteia*', in Silk (ed.), *Tragedy and the Tragic*, p. 134.

46. Schopenhauer, *The World as Will and Representation*, vol. 2, p. 349.

47. Ibid., vol. 1, p. 322.

48. Ibid., vol. 2, p. 357.

49. Ibid., vol. 1, p. 196.

50. Ibid., vol. 2, p. 578.

51. See Søren Kierkegaard, *Fear and Trembling* (Harmondsworth, 1987), esp. *Problema 1*.

52. For a somewhat implausible defence of the Dionysian, one which largely fails to note that it is terroristic as well as life-yielding, see Paul Gordon, *Tragedy after Nietzsche* (Urbana, IL and Chicago, 2001). See also Peter Sloterdijk, *Thinker on Stage: Nietzsche's Materialism* (Minneapolis, MN, 1989). For a close textual analysis of *The Birth of Tragedy*, see Paul de Man, *Allegories of Reading* (New Haven, CT and London, 1979), ch. 4.

53. Nietzsche, *The Joyful Wisdom*, p. 266.

54. Nietzsche, *Ecce Homo*, in Kaufmann (ed.), *Basic Writings of Nietzsche*, p. 785.

55. Deleuze, *Nietzsche and Philosophy*, p. 17.

56. Quoted by W.B. Yeats, *Essays and Introductions* (New York, 1961), p. 523.

57. Nietzsche, *The Birth of Tragedy*, in Kaufmann (ed.), *Basic Writings of Nietzsche*, p. 104. For a close study of Nietzsche's text, see Paul Raimond Daniels, *Nietzsche and the Birth of Tragedy* (Stocksfield, 2013).

58. Slavoj Žižek, *The Puppet and the Dwarf* (London, 2003), p. 81.

59. Quoted in Kaufmann, *Basic Writings on Nietzsche*, p. 728.

60. See, for example, Heidegger's discussion of *Oedipus Tyrannus* in his *Introduction to Metaphysics* (New Haven, CT and London, 2000), pp. 112–14.

61. Georg Lukács, *Soul and Form* (London, 1974), p. 162.
62. See 'Tragedy and the Whole Truth', in Aldous Huxley, *Music at Night* (London, 1931).
63. Kenneth Buke, *Counter-Statement* (New York, 1931), p. 42.
64. Krutch, *The Modern Temper*, p. 125.
65. Ibid., p. 126.
66. Gordon, *Tragedy after Nietzsche*, p. 18.
67. Arthur Miller, 'Tragedy and the Common Man', p. 4.
68. Theodor Adorno, *Noten zur Literatur* (Frankfurt am Main, 1974), p. 423.
69. Sands, 'Tragedy, Theology, and Feminism', p. 83.
70. Georg Simmel, 'On the Concept and Tragedy of Culture', in K. Peter Etzkorn (ed.), *Georg Simmel: The Conflict in Modern Culture and Other Essays* (New York, 1968), p. 46.
71. See Franz Rosenzweig, *The Star of Redemption* (London, 1971), p. 211.
72. For a valuable account of Brecht's rejection of tragedy, see Raymond Williams, *Modern Tragedy*, Part 2, ch. 7.
73. See Alain Robbe-Grillet, *For a New Novel* (Freeport, NY, 1970), p. 59.
74. Quoted by Gordon, *Tragedy after Nietzsche*, p. 86.
75. Theodor Adorno, *Prisms* (London, 1967), p. 32.
76. John Haffenden, *William Empson*, vol. 1: *Among the Mandarins* (Oxford, 2005), p. 204.
77. D. Porter (ed.), *The Seminar of Jacques Lacan*, Book 7: *The Ethics of Psychoanalysis* (New York, 1986), pp. 249–50.
78. See Žižek's essay 'A Plea for Ethical Violence', in the online journal *The Bible and Critical Theory*, vol. 1, no. 1 (Monash University Epress).
79. William Desmond, *Perplexity and Ultimacy* (New York, 1995), pp. 30, 32 and 49.
80. See Billings, *Genealogy of the Tragic*, p. 1.
81. Raymond Williams, *Modern Tragedy*, p. 27.
82. See Michelle Gellrich, *Tragedy and Theory* (Princeton, NJ, 1988).
83. See Lawrence E. Klein, *Shaftesbury and the Culture of Politeness* (Cambridge, 1994), pp. 187–8. For tragic ideas in the medieval period, see Henry Ansgard Kelly, *Ideas and Forms of Tragedy* (Cambridge, 1993).
84. Rowan Williams, *The Tragic Imagination*, p, 47.
85. See Rowan Williams, 'Trinity and Ontology', in Kenneth Surin (ed.), *Christ, Ethics and Tragedy* (Cambridge, 1989), pp. 78 and 85.

INDEX

Abel, Lionel, 16
Absolute, the, 25, 35, 78, 170,
 171, 174, 175, 176, 181, 182
absolute value, 75, 126
Adorno, Theodor, 172, 211,
 213
Aeschylus: *Eumenides*, 2; *Oresteia*,
 17, 47, 66–7, 88, 189;
 Prometheus Bound, 67, 68; *The
 Suppliants*, 65
aesthetics, 171–3, 174, 193–4,
 197–202
Albee, Edward, *Who's Afraid of
 Virginia Woolf?* 154
alterity, 63
Althusser, Louis, 108–11, 111
American tragedy, 98 *see also*
 Miller, Arthur; O'Neill, Eugene;
 Williams, Tennessee
Anderson, Perry, 88
Anouihl, Jean, 36, 127
anthropocentrism, 106

Antigone (Sophocles), 35–8, 47–8,
 65, 78, 81, 83, 177, 186, 190
Apollonian, the, 195, 200–1, 205
Aquinas, Thomas, 33
Arendt, Hannah, 2, 3
Aristophanes, 11
Aristotle, 4, 17, 23, 24, 158, 159,
 172, 189, 215
Arnold, Matthew, 102; *Empedocles
 on Etna*, 83
art-work, unity of, 163–5
Athenian humanism, 62
Auerbach, Eric, 54

Barthes, Roland, 10, 45, 213
Beckett, Samuel, 22, 97; *Waiting
 for Godot*, 143
Beistegui, Miguel de, 156, 184
Benjamin, Walter, 21, 24, 39, 59,
 84–6, 212
Billings, Joshua, 60, 82, 83, 214
blindness, 54, 64, 111–12, 145

235

Bolt, Robert, *A Man for All Seasons*, 127

bourgeois tragedy, 8, 94, 96, 138–9

bourgeoisie, 91, 94, 95–6, 138, 162, 167, 189 *see also* middle classes

Bradley, A.C., 28, 188–9

Brecht, Bertolt, 9, 38, 97, 212

Brontë, Emily, *Wuthering Heights*, 48

Büchner, Georg: *Danton's Death*, 80; *Woyzeck*, 21

Burke, Edmund, 9, 66–7, 102

Burke, Kenneth, 209

Calderón, Pedro, *Life Is a Dream*, 134

Camus, Albert, 16, 57, 98, 178, 212

Cervantes, Miguel de, *Don Quixote*, 57

Chekhov, Anton, 89–90, 97, 141–2; *The Cherry Orchard*, 89, 142; *The Seagull*, 141; *Three Sisters*, 141, 142; *Uncle Vanya*, 141, 142

Chorus, in Greek tragedy, 2, 59, 65

Christianity, 16, 17–19, 29, 37, 66, 82, 105, 178–9, 204–5

Coetzee, J.M., *Waiting for the Barbarians*, 34

colonialism and anti-colonialism, 19

comédie noire, 45, 152

comedy, 26, 133, 149, 187–8, 192, 219

Condorcet, Nicolas de, 107

conflict, 19, 27, 60, 77, 94, 155–6, 159, 179, 189, 218

Conrad, Joseph, 128–31; *The Heart of Darkness*, 129; *Lord Jim*, 128–9, 131; *Nostromo*, 110, 129–30; *The Secret Agent*, 130–1; *Typhoon*, 131

consciousness, 108, 111

consolation, 12, 102, 169, 220

Constant, Benjamin, 92

Corneille, Pierre: *Cinna*, 187; *Le Cid*, 187

Critchley, Simon, 76, 171

death drive, 167, 175–6 *see also* Thanatos

Deleuze, Gilles, 19, 122, 203

demonic, 217–18

Derrida, Jacques, 172, 207

desire, 30, 71

Desmond, William, 214

determinism, 12, 106, 108, 160 *see also* fate

dialectics, 184

Dickens, Charles, 93

Diderot, Denis, 8

Dionysian, the, 83, 183, 195, 200–1, 203, 205

Dionysus, festival of, 2, 197

divine law, 79

Dostoevsky, Fyodor, *Crime and Punishment*, 95

Eliot, George, *Middlemarch*, 39

Eliot, T.S.: *The Cocktail Party*, 151, 152–4; *The Family Reunion*, 151, 152–3; *Murder in the Cathedral*, 151–2; *The Reunion*, 91

empathy, 188–9, 195
Empson, William, 14, 125, 213
Engels, Friedrich, 84
Enlightenment rationalism, 169
epistemophilia, 131–2
Eros, 35, 46, 71, 78, 175, 200,
   211
Es, Bart van, 70
Eumenides, 68
Euripides, 12, 15, 66, 74, 158, 171
Europe, political revolution, 80
exchange-value, 71–2, 73
Expressionist theatre, 97

Fall, the, 49
false consciousness, 99, 105, 111,
   112, 116, 131, 134, 147, 153,
   198
falsehood, 112, 117–18, 140
family, the, 46–7, 137–8
fate, 15, 28, 52, 62, 78, 84, 85,
   92, 159, 173, 174, 177–8, 179,
   208, 212, 215 *see also*
   determinism; necessity
Feher, Ferenc, 16
Felski, Rita, 29
Fitzgerald, Scott, *The Great Gatsby*,
   129, 150
Ford, John, *'Tis Pity She's a Whore*,
   48
Foucault, Michel, 88, 119
France, seventeenth-century
   politics, 79
freedom: and determinism, 106,
   108, 110; in Ibsen and
   Chekhov, 89–90, 92–3, 96,
   135; and necessity, 159–61,
   163–5, 167, 171–9

French Revolution, 81, 102, 166,
   176–7, 183
Freud, Sigmund, 15, 33, 51, 107,
   110, 113–14, 120, 200, 201,
   211
Friedrich, Rainer, 3, 82
Friel, Brian, *Translations*, 143
Furies, 68, 189

Gardner, Helen, 156
Geist, 184, 186
Gellrich, Michelle, 215–16
genetics, 108
German Idealism, 81, 164, 177,
   179, 183, 189, 198
Germany: tragic drama, 3, 21, 24,
   59, 79–80; tragic theory, 158,
   183, 214
Gibbon, Edward, 103
God (Christian), 66, 103, 181–2;
   absent, 75–6; death of, 6, 16,
   105
gods, Olympian, 66
Goethe, Johann Wolfgang von:
   Egmont, 79, 83, 191; *Faust*, 190;
   Götz von Berlichingen, 79, 83;
   Iphigenia in Tauris, 79, 191;
   Torquato Tasso, 79; *Wilhelm
   Meister*, 3
Goldhill, Simon, 24, 60, 159
Golding, William, *Free Fall*, 68
Goldmann, Lucien, 75–6, 79
Goncourt, Edmond de, 7–8
Goncourt, Jules de, 7–8
Gorgias the Sophist, 122
Goux, Jean-Joseph, 63
Gramsci, Antonio, 66
Gray, John, 117

Greek tragedy, 2–4, 9, 23, 24, 28–9, 33, 40, 58, 59, 65–6, 81, 82, 83, 87, 162, 177, 186, 208, 212
Gregory, Augusta, 203
Gulag, the, 32

Haffenden, John, 213
Halliday, Stephen, 81
Halpern, Richard, 15
Hardy, Thomas, 95, 187; *Jude the Obscure*, 20
Hebbel, Friedrich, 185
Hegel, Georg Wilhelm Friedrich, 9, 15, 19, 24, 27–8, 31, 38, 63, 67, 81–2, 95, 112, 127, 169, 170–1, 178, 183–90, 199, 203, 216
hegemony, 66, 67, 102, 164
Heidegger, Martin, 86, 89, 125, 171, 172, 207, 208–9
Heller, Agnes, 16
Herder, Johann Gottfried, 69
hero, death of, 82–3
hero, tragic: bourgeois, 8; as entrepreneur, 93–4; and illusion, 143–4; inner conflict, 26–7, 168; mythological, 59; and optimism, 210; and Platonic ideal, 215; and rationality, 76, 79; sacrificial death, 84–5, 174–5, 178, 180, 181, 203–4; as signifier, 149; and theology, 17; *see also* protagonist, tragic
Hitler, Adolf, 86
Hölderlin, Friedrich, 21, 23, 165, 169, 171, 178, 179–80, 181–3,

214; *The Death of Empedocles*, 80, 83
Holocaust, the, 10, 16, 32–3, 172
Horace, 29
Hoxby, Blair, 1, 58
hubris, 178
human action, 54, 110
human agency, 65
humanism, 62
humanity, 64–5
Hume, David, 9, 102, 103, 108, 115–16
Huxley, Aldous, 209
hysteric, the, 76

Ibsen, Henrik, 4–5, 89–97, 135–40, 148; *Brand*, 78, 91, 95; *A Doll's House*, 93, 138; *An Enemy of the People*, 14, 135; *Hedda Gabler*, 95; *John Gabriel Borkman*, 95, 97, 136–7, 139, 140; *The Master Builder*, 95; *The Pillars of the Community*, 91, 94, 139; *Rosemersholm*, 90, 92, 97, 140; *When We Dead Awaken*, 93, 95, 96, 97; *The Wild Duck*, 136
identity, instability of, 41–3, 71–2
ideology, 86, 99, 101, 108, 109, 113, 115, 198, 220
illusion, 132–4, 140, 154
incest, 43–54, 63, 67, 73, 78, 98, 132, 226n6
indeterminacy, 55
individualism, 12, 24, 27, 74–5, 91, 138, 183, 185, 189, 194–5
irony, 42, 44

Jacobean tragedy, 69, 74–5
James, Henry, 'The Beast in the Jungle', 1
Jameson, Fredric, 88
Jefferson, Thomas, 103
Jesus, 179 *see also* Christianity

Kane, Sarah, *Phaedra's Love*, 138
Kant, Immanuel, 24, 63, 103, 108, 111, 162–3, 165–6, 168, 170–1, 172, 173, 193
Kaufmann, Walter, 158
Kermode, Frank, 118
Kierkegaard, Søren, 27, 37, 197
kinship, 42, 44–5, 73
Kleist, Heinrich von, 21; *Penthesilea*, 79; *Prince Friedrich von Homburg*, 79–80
knowledge, 51, 60–1, 62, 87, 131–2
Krutch, Joseph Wood, 16, 209–10

Lacan, Jacques, 9, 32, 35, 36, 98, 113, 199–200, 214, 224–5n59
Lasalle, Ferdinand de, *Franz von Sickingen*, 84
Law, the, 67, 85
Lear, King, 14, 17, 54
Leavis, F.R., 133
Lehrer, Tom, 45–6
Lessing, Gotthold, 3, 8
liberalism, 93, 155
liminal states: and tragedy, 56–7, 70 *see also* transition
literary fiction, 128
love, 78, 175

Lukács, Georg, 57–8, 86, 171, 172, 209
lying, 101, 111, 116

Machiavelli, Niccolò, 114–15, 116
MacKinnon, Donald, 217
Macmurray, John, 160
Magris, Claudio, 57
Maistre, Joseph-Marie de, 103
Mann, Thomas, *The Holy Sinner*, 48
Marx, Karl, 19, 23, 71, 83–4, 112–13, 136, 160, 189, 190, 211
Marxism, 17–19
McCabe, Richard, 44
McGuinness, Frank, *Observe the Sons of Ulster*, 100–1
meaning, 32–3, 46, 58, 60–1, 69–70, 72, 74–5, 87, 169, 218
Megill, Allan, 171
Melville, Hermann, *Moby Dick*, 126
Merleau-Ponty, Maurice, 40
middle classes, 94, 156–7, 158, 160, 161, 166 *see also* bourgeoisie
Mill, John Stuart, 155
Miller, Arthur, 29, 210; *Death of a Salesman*, 34–5, 78, 138, 149–50; *A View from the Bridge*, 50, 126, 151, 177
Miller, Jacques-Alain, 127–8, 149
mimesis, 60
modernism, 34, 88–9, 97, 121, 128, 198
modernity, 5, 29–31, 38, 58, 159, 189

monsters/monstrosity, 49–50, 63
Montaigne, Michel de, 103
Moretti, Franco, 46, 69, 94
Müntzer, Thomas, 84
Murdoch, Iris, 113; *A Severed
    Head*, 45
Musil, Robert, *The Man Without
    Qualities*, 112
mystery, 169
myth, 59–60, 86, 99–100, 124

nationhood, 102
nation-states, 69, 87
Nature, 65, 182
necessity, 159–61, 163–5, 167,
    169, 171–9 *see also*
    determinism; fate
neuroscience, 108
New Testament, 205
Nietzsche, Friedrich, 15, 22, 28,
    94–5, 103, 105, 110, 111, 113,
    116–23, 165, 171–2, 178, 185,
    188, 194–5, 197–207, 214;
    Beyond Good and Evil, 117; *The
    Birth of Tragedy*, 51, 120, 121,
    199; *Ecce Homo*, 206; *The
    Genealogy of Morals*, 117, 118;
    The Joyful Wisdom, 117, 121,
    203; *Thus Spake Zarathustra*,
    119; *The Twilight of the Idols*,
    197; *Untimely Meditations*, 38;
    The Will to Power, 105, 118, 121
nihilism, 20–1, 197, 206
Norris, Christopher, 13
novel, the, 57–8

O'Casey, Sean, *Juno and the
    Paycock*, 143

Oedipus complex, 15
O'Neill, Eugene, 30, 33; *The
    Iceman Cometh*, 146–8; *Long
    Day's Journey into Night*, 145–6
order, sense of, 69, 70–1, 73
original sin, 31, 54, 91–2, 101,
    195
Other, the, 30, 42–3, 47, 60–1, 76

parricide, 40, 52
Pascal, *Pensées*, 103
Pasternak, Boris, *Doctor Zhivago*,
    10
Paul, St, 85, 181–2
philosophy, 63, 81, 162, 170–2,
    184, 206–7, 214
philosophy of tragedy, 80–1, 172,
    215
Pinter, Harold, *The Caretaker*, 141
Pirandello, Luigi, *Henry IV*, 133
pity and fear, 13, 156, 189
Plato, 4, 42, 81, 100–1, 106, 110,
    116, 171, 215
plurality, 41
polis, 2–3, 42, 46, 59, 60, 68, 82,
    87, 98, 176
politics, and tragedy, 2–5, 79–80,
    87
postmodernism, 16, 41, 126,
    218–19
power, 66–8, 101–3, 114–15,
    134
pragmatism, 118
protagonist, tragic: bourgeois, 7–8,
    127; and Christianity, 18,
    178–9; and death drive, 78; and
    fate, 174–5, 178–9; and
    freedom, 168; Ibsenite, 92–6,

135; and modernity, 28–9, 34–5, 150–1; partial knowledge of, 60; Platonic ideal, 215; Romantic, 91; sacrificial death, 84–6, 178–82, 203–4; and self-responsibility, 27; and transcendence, 75; and truth-telling, 148; *see also* hero, tragic

Protestantism, 79

psychoanalytic theory, 29–30, 113–14

Racine, Jean, 15, 57, 75–9; *Andromache*, 77; *Britannicus*, 77; *Phèdre*, 77, 78

rationalism, 169

Real, the, 9, 18, 35, 38, 50, 113, 114, 120, 126, 149, 199, 200, 224–5n59

Realpolitik, 70, 83

reconciliation, 88, 155–8, 173, 180, 183, 187, 189, 190–1, 201, 214, 218

Reiss, Timothy J., 87–8

religion, 103–5, 115

Renan, Ernest, 102

republicanism, 83; and tragedy, 23

resignation, 175, 195

revenge, 69, 73, 75

revolution, 83, 84, 87

Richards, I.A., 125, 139, 156, 157

Richardson, Samuel, *Clarissa*, 17, 78

riddles, 40, 45–6, 48, 60, 63

Rilke, Rainer Maria: 'Requiem,' 193; *Sonnet to Orpheus*, 209

Robbe-Grillet, Alain, 212–13

Roberts, John, 112

Robinson, Marilynne, *Housekeeping*, 140

Romanticism, 87, 91, 159, 189

Rosenzweig, Franz, 212

Rousseau, Jean-Jacques, 176

Rymer, Thomas, *A Short View of Tragedy* (1693), 28

sacrificial death, 82–3, 84–6, 173, 184–5

Sands, Kathleen M., 18

Santner, Eric, 47

scapegoats, 86

Scheler, Max, 162–3

Schelling, Friedrich, 26–7, 80, 161, 165, 171, 173–4, 176–7, 178, 214

Schiller, Friedrich, 165, 167–8, 173, 214; *The Conspiracy of Fiesco in Genoa*, 79; *Don Carlos*, 79, 80, 173; *Maria Stuart*, 79, 173; *The Robbers*, 78, 79, 173; *Wallenstein*, 79, 102–3, 135, 173, 183

Schlegel, A.W., 174

Schlegel, Friedrich, 164

Schmidt, Dennis, 162, 185

Schmitt, Carl, 24, 69, 104

Schopenhauer, Arthur, 6–7, 34, 110, 111, 117, 171, 187, 191–7, 202

science, 160

Scruton, Roger, 111

Segal, Charles, 58

self, the, 52–3, 60, 62, 64, 72, 73, 110, 113, 127–8, 159, 161–2, 177, 207

self, transcendent, 166

self-determination, 52–4, 60, 64, 71, 72–3, 91–2, 93, 160–2
self-estrangement, 61
self-knowledge, 52
self-surrender, 176
sexuality, 47
Shaftesbury, Earl of, 216
Shakespeare, William: and illusion, 132–4; tragedies, 27–8, 69–70, 74; *Antony and Cleopatra*, 48, 175; *Coriolanus*, 53; *Hamlet*, 17, 70, 73, 98, 133, 150; *King Lear*, 14, 17, 54, 64, 72, 133; *Macbeth*, 72, 134; *Measure for Measure*, 175, 194; *A Midsummer Night's Dream*, 41, 71; *Othello*, 133, 158; *The Tempest*, 133–4; *Timon of Athens*, 20–1, 71; *Troilus and Cressida*, 72, 73; *Twelfth Night*, 71
Simmel, Georg, 211–12
Skinner, Quentin, 115
social order, 3, 5, 30, 36, 50, 71, 73, 76, 85, 87, 101, 109
Socrates, 15, 19, 171, 206
Solger, Karl, 181
Sombart, Werner, 94
Sontag, Susan, 16
Sophocles, 10; *Ajax*, 67; *Antigone*, 35–6, 37–8, 47–8, 65, 78, 81, 83, 177, 186, 190; *Oedipus at Colonus*, 2, 54–5; *Oedipus Tyrannus*, 40–51, 58–65, 78, 131–2, 162, 174; *Philoctetes*, 78
Sorel, Georges, 124, 125
sovereignty, 67, 101
Sparks, Simon, 156
Spengler, Oswald, 212

Sphinx, the, 40, 44–5, 47–8, 50, 60, 63, 64, 65
Spinoza, Baruch, 106–9, 111
Spirit, 81–2, 178, 180, 184, 185, 186, 187
statecraft, 68
Steiner, George, 5, 8–9, 14, 15–16, 17, 20–2, 38, 76, 159, 223n41
Stevens, Wallace, 125
Strauss, Leo, 104
Strindberg, August: *Dance of Death*, 137; *Easter*, 90; *The Father*, 61, 90, 140
subjectivity, 73, 76, 111, 161–2, 192–3, 196
sublime, the, 165–70
suffering, 202–6
suicide, 64, 97
symbolic order, 35, 37, 41, 44, 46, 50, 73, 132
Synge, J.M.: *The Playboy of the Western World*, 142–4; *The Well of the Saints*, 112, 145
Szondi, Peter, 184

Thanatos, 35, 50, 78, 135, 175, 185, 200, 211
theatre, 132–4
theodicy, 183, 202
Tillyard, E.M.W., 69
Toland, John, 103
tragedy, and real-life events, 10–11, 32
tragic culture, 28, 207–8
tragic vision, 11, 19, 79, 149, 159, 172, 197, 207, 209
tragic world-view, 10, 159

transcendence, 5, 22, 74, 75
transcendent self, 166
transition, and tragedy, 57–9, 79–80, 81–8, 96–8
Trauerspiel playwrights, 21, 24, 59, 212
truth: absence of, 198; and authenticity, 125–6; and ethics, 126–7; and experience, 108–9; and extremity, 34; and false consciousness, 116, 130–1; and falsehood, 111–14; and family, 137–8; and identity, 42–3, 54, 61, 150; and illusion, 128–9, 140, 154; and myth, 124–5; and Nietzsche, 116–23, 137; and power, 102–3; and reconciliation, 155; and virtue, 114–15

Übermensch, 95, 105, 120, 122–3, 200, 202
unity, in tragic art, 167, 173–4, 180, 182, 183, 188, 218
unity of opposites, 77, 220
unity of the self, 110

Vaihinger, Hans, 124
value, 20, 32, 33, 72, 75–6, 79, 218 *see also* exchange-value

Vernant, Jean-Pierre, 2, 24, 59, 61, 62
Vidal-Naquet, Pierre, 2, 59, 61, 62
virtue, 3, 113, 114, 218
Vischer, Friedrich, 181, 185
Voltaire, 103, 116

Wagner, Richard, 21
Wallace, Jennifer, 98
Weber, Max, 31, 88, 104
Wilde, Oscar, 110–11, 124, 125
Will, the, 110, 191–6, 204
Williams, Bernard, 24, 65
Williams, Raymond, viii, 16–17, 19, 23, 25, 56, 70, 93, 141, 214–15
Williams, Rowan, 217
Williams, Tennessee, 148
Wittgenstein, Ludwig, 72, 158, 167
World Trade Center attacks, 2001, 11

Yeats, W.B., 124, 125, 189

Zeus, 66, 68
Žižek, Slavoj, 32, 33, 35–6, 38, 114, 204, 214